NY NIGHTLIFE

Photos of the stars at night in
Max's Kansas City,
The Mudd Club,
Studio 54,
CBGBs,
Area
and other places where I forget I was.

All text, photos art direction
and design by George DuBose

An imprint of Wonderland Publishing, LLC

NY Nightlife
Photos of the stars at night in Max's Kansas City,
The Mudd College of Deviant Behavior, Studio 54,
CBGBs, Area and other places where I forget I was.
First Edition
ISBN 978-0-9863-0458-3

Cover photo of Jean-Michel Basquiat
by George DuBose

Printed by Kindle Direct Worldwide
Library of Congress cataloging-in-publication data
All of the images in this book are available
as signed, numbered limited edition fine art prints.
for more information contact: boss@george-dubose.com

Other books from Wonderland Publishing, LLC

"I Speak Music	- Ramones"	English Edition	ISBN 978-0-9889-2340-9
"Hablo Musica	- Ramones"	Españoles Edición	ISBN 978-0-9889-2341-6
"Eu Falo Música	- Ramones"	Português Edição	ISBN 978-0-9889-2345-4
"Parlo Musica	- Ramones"	Edizione Italiana	ISBN 978-0-9889-2347-8
"I Speak Music	- Hip Hop - Old School Volume One"		ISBN 978-0-9889-2342-3
"I Speak Music	- Hip Hop - Old School Volume Two"		ISBN 978-0-9889-2343-0
"I Speak Music	- Hip Hop - Old School Volume Three"		ISBN 978-0-9889-2344-7
"The Big Book of Hip-Hop Photography"		First Edition	ISBN 978-0-9889-2346-1
"Renovate a Sailboat and Cross the Atlantic"		First Edition	ISBN 978-0-9889-2348-5
"Madonna - Raw"	- English version	First Edition	ISBN 978-0-9863-0451-4
"Madonna - Raw"	- Edizione Italiana	First Edition	ISBN 978-0-9863-0452-1
"Madonna - Raw"	- German version	First Edition	ISBN 978-0-9863-0453-8
"Madonna - Raw"	- Españoles Edición	First Edition	ISBN 978-0-9863-0454-5
"My Best Shot"		First Edition	ISBN 978-0-9863-0455-2
"Klaus Nomi - A Cult Icon"		First Edition	ISBN 978-0-9863-0456-9

When I was discharged from the US Navy, I knew that I wanted to become a portrait photographer in the vein of Yousef Karsch of Ottawa, whose WW2 photo of Winston Churchill had inspired me.

I thought my path to greatness would start at a photography school in Manhattan. I moved to Edgewater, NJ and enrolled in the Germain School of Photography. I quickly learned that the first year of a two year program would be photography theory and darkroom techniques. I had already taught myself to develop B&W negative and color slide films. I wanted to learn studio lighting.

I went to bartender's school hoping to keep myself financially afloat, but the first job I got was washing dishes in an Italian restaurant.

Eventually, I answered a printing company's newpaper ad for a "cameraman", only to learn that this was no camera I had ever seen, it was 20 feet long and made the printing plates for the presses. I began to learn a lot about printing...

Finally, a pal of my uncle's, who was a fashion photographer, gave me a list of all the photo studios in NY. I started making phone calls, looking for a photo assistant's position, but the phone was usually the studio assistant who hung up on me. I resorted to knocking on doors, only to have the assistants slam the door in my face.

My first break was when Lane Pederson and his partner, Jim Erwin ran a catalog studio and hired me to pack merchandise and move boxes. As the third assistant, I wasn't allowed to touch the cameras.

I kept my job at the printing company in New Jersey and after my eight hour night shift, I would go into Manhattan and work eight more hours for Lane and Jim. At Christmas, they laid off all the assistants, but in January, they called me and offered me a full-time job, with no layoffs.

One of the perks was that I had keys to the studio, the combination to the camera safe and was allowed to use all the film and paper I wanted for building my portfolio. I began taking their Nikons out to a Brooklyn jazz club to photograph the musicians performing there and would give the club owner a print from every artist I photographed.

Another perk was that Lane and Jim were constantly getting invitations to parties and exhibitions. They rarely went to these events and offered the invitations to me.

I remember going to a photo exhibit by Christopher Makos, who was Man Ray's assistant at one time. Christopher made 8 x 10" prints and placed them on the floor of the gallery, covering the prints with clear plexiglass.
The name of the exhibit was "Step On It".

There I met Richard Cramer, the assistant art director of Andy Warhol's "Interview" magazine. Richard and I became friends, sharing similar interests in new music. Richard began to ask me to shoot young models wearing various t-shirts promoting Andy's movies. I also began to process Andy's 35mm films that he shot at the parties he went to.

One day in 1977, Richard called me and asked me if I wanted to go to Max's Kansas City, a music bar/restaurant to see a band from Georgia. As I had lived in Atlanta in my youth, I was curious. I told Richard that my payday was several days away and I was broke and had no money for a ticket.

Richard said, "No problem, you will be on the band's guest list.

MAX'S KANSAS CITY NYC

So I was on my first guest list at Max's Kansas City. I had visited Max's since my first visits to New York when I was still in college. In the early 70s, Max's hosted folk music artists, but by the late 70s, Max's was showcasing the up-and-coming punk and new wave bands. I never saw the Ramones' early gigs there, but I saw the "B52s" and what was supposed to be Klaus Nomi's first stage performance.

The first band was Lydia Lunch and her band was called "Teenage Jesus and the Jerks". Up to this time I had had little experience with punk rock and didn't understand the minimalistic philosophy of that genre.

The next band was the band I came to see. Before they came on stage, there was a buzzing sound like bees. Then, when the band picked up their instruments, they start off playing the "Theme From Peter Gunn", a television show popular in the 1950s that my parents would watch as I was tucked into bed. That was the first melody I could pick out on my first guitar. I couldn't tune the guitar, but I could pick out the three notes of the bass line. The "B52s" song was "Planet Claire". I fell in love and imagined if I had kept playing the guitar, I would want to be in this band.

I asked the band if they would come to my bosses' studio and let me take a photograph to show "Interview" magazine. When the band showed up minus Cindy Wilson, who had gone back to Athens, Georgia, I got Maureen McLaughlin, their manager at the time, to stand in.

"Interview" used the "wrong" photo. Then licensed my "B52s" photo to a Japanese magazine. When I finally bribed the band with piña coladas and banana daiquiris to come to "my" studio , I tried to get them to pose like the cover of the "Ventures'" "Walk, Don't Run 64" inspired by the 60s fashion of the girl on the cover and the fact that Ricky Wilson played a "Ventures'" model Mosrite guitar.

In the end, the band chose a more boring line up photo. I used that photo and some Japanese characters from the Japanese "B52s" article and printed 500 16 x 20" prints and would tape them to mailboxes or whatever around the club where the band was scheduled to perform.

Two years on, the band got a record deal with Chris Blackwell of Island Records, Sue Absurd aka Tony Wright, bought the rights to use my photo for the cover of the yellow album and thc rest is history.

Lydia Lunch, the leader of "Teenage Jesus and The Jerks" played minimalistic, atonal and very short songs. I still didn't "get" this punk thing.

Ricky Wilson, the "B52s" guitarist played a Mosrite guitar made famous by the California surf rock band "The Ventures". When I once asked Ricky why his guitar only had five strings, he told me that

when he was learning to play, often when he broke a string, he couldn't afford to buy new ones. The "B52s" also used an old Farfisa keyboard that gave their songs a real '60s flavor.

Here you see that Ricky's guitar is missing the "G" string.

Here, Fred Schneider, is playing an old cassette player.

Not too many rock bands played bongo drums. That the band used an old Farfisa organ, an old Mosrite guitar, toy pianos really gave the "B52's" a new, but almost classic sound.

Kate Pearson played the Farfisa keyboard
and also a guitar with six strings.

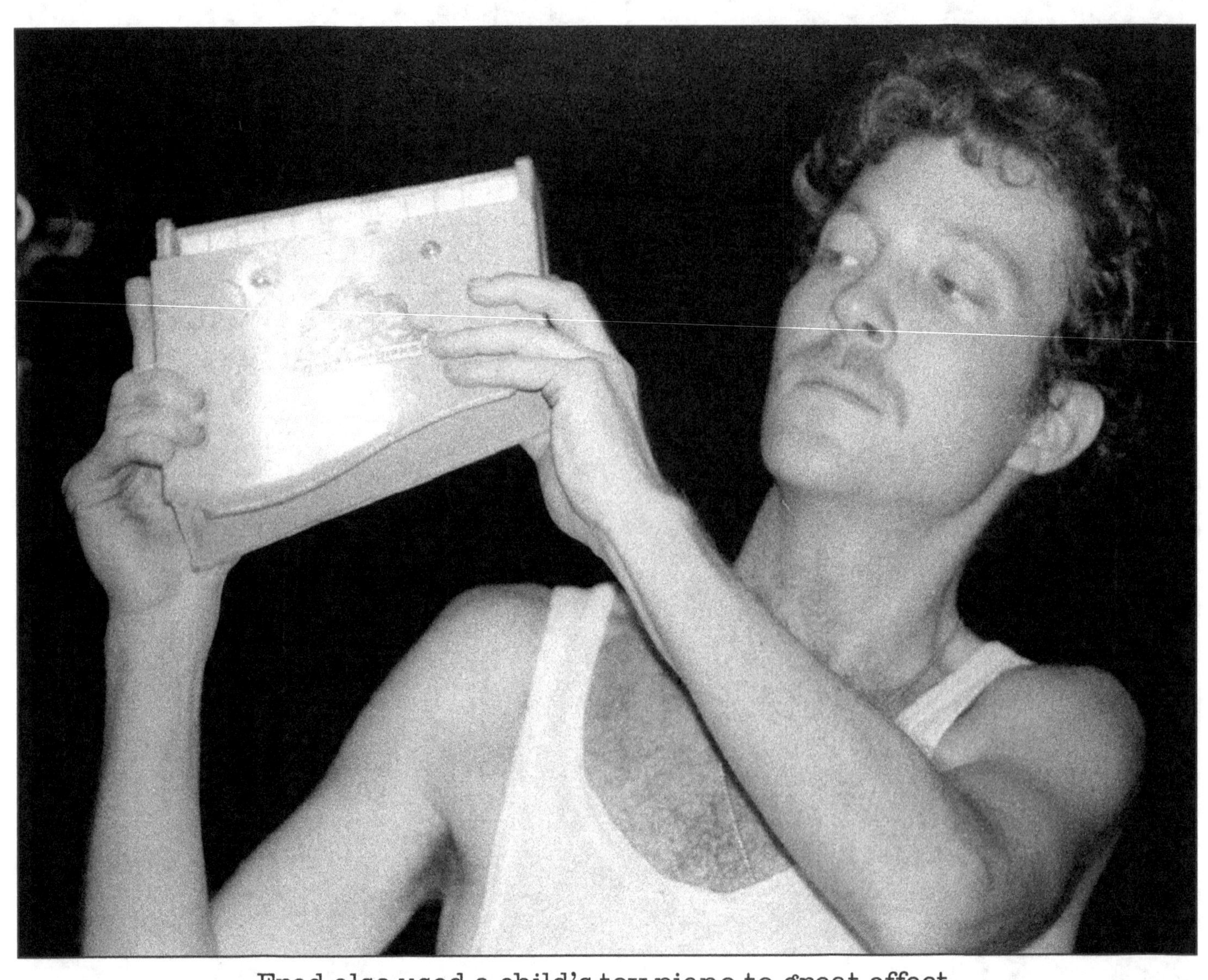

Fred also used a child's toy piano to great effect.

When the “B52s” came back to NY, I went to see them again and again. I told them I needed a photo for “Interview”. Cindy Wilson had left for Athens, Georgia, so I asked Maureen, their manager to stand in.

When the band returned to NY the third time, I was able to get them to “my” studio and tried to recreate The Ventures “Walk, Don’t Run ‘64”. The girls styled themselves like the woman on that Ventures album cover.

I gave this photo to “Interview” for Glenn O’Brien’s article. The band didn’t care for my Ventures’ inspiration. I made a 16 x 20” poster and printed 500 copies, taping them to mailboxes near their venue. I didn’t know to use wheat paste as glue and the posters were stolen as fast as I could put them up.

THE MUDD COLLEGE OF DEVIANT BEHAVIOR

When I was still working as a photographer's apprentice, after my day at the Pederson-Erwin catalog studio, I would take the #6 subway uptown to 86th Street, stop at the Papaya King, buy my two hotdogs and a papaya drink and that was my dinner for $2.50. Sometimes, I would have leftover sandwiches that the fashion models didn't finish. I was making $125 a week and my apartment rent was $300 a month. so it was a forced economy.

I would get to my apartment on Second Avenue and 89th street and take a "disco nap" from 1830 to 2300 and then get back on the #6 subway and head downtown to Canal Street. Dave's Luncheonette was on the corner of Canal and Broadway. I would have a potato knish with mustard and a cherry Coke. Knishes were great for sucking up alcohol.

After getting past whoever was working the door at the Mudd Club, I would party until 0400, take the #6 train back uptown and finish my "disco nap" and get back downtown to the photo studio by 0900.

I would go to the Mudd Club every night, unless there was a band, party or event at another location.

I saw Marianne Faithfull, Joe Jackson, Was, Not Was and of course the "B52s". When I was photographing Joe Jackson at what was his first US appearance, there was a lady who came up to me and told me that she would pay me $75 for a photo of Joe on stage.

After Jackson's performance, I went back to the Pederson-Erwin studio, processed the B&W films, made contact sheets and took the #6 home. When I got back to the studio the next morning, I asked Mr. Pederson, if I could deliver some contact sheets to A&M Records at lunchtime. As we weren't shooting that morning, Lane told me to deliver the contact sheets immediately.

I think I shocked the lady from the Mudd Club the previous night, who turned out to be the national director of publicity for A&M. That was my "foot in the door" and Kathy Schenker gave me many assignments until I started working as the photo editor at SPIN magazine.

So the "B52s" and Joe Jackson got my career up and running.

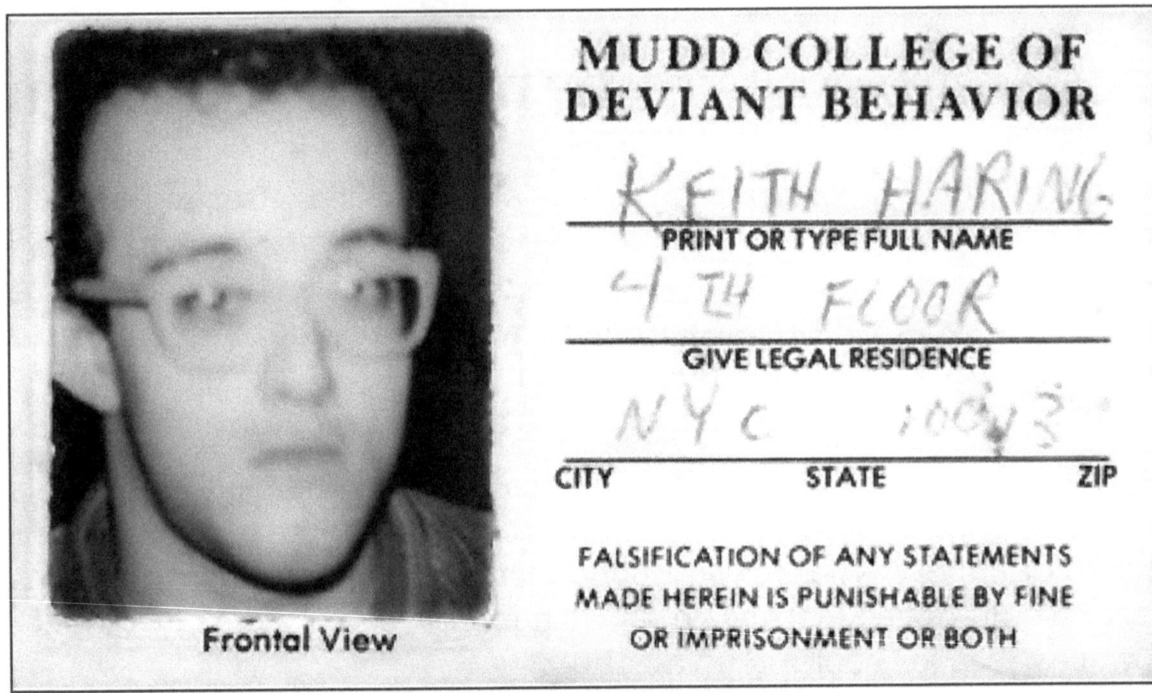

MUDD COLLEGE OF DEVIANT BEHAVIOR

KEITH HARING

PRINT OR TYPE FULL NAME

4 TH FLOOR

GIVE LEGAL RESIDENCE

NYC

CITY STATE ZIP

FALSIFICATION OF ANY STATEMENTS MADE HEREIN IS PUNISHABLE BY FINE OR IMPRISONMENT OR BOTH

Frontal View

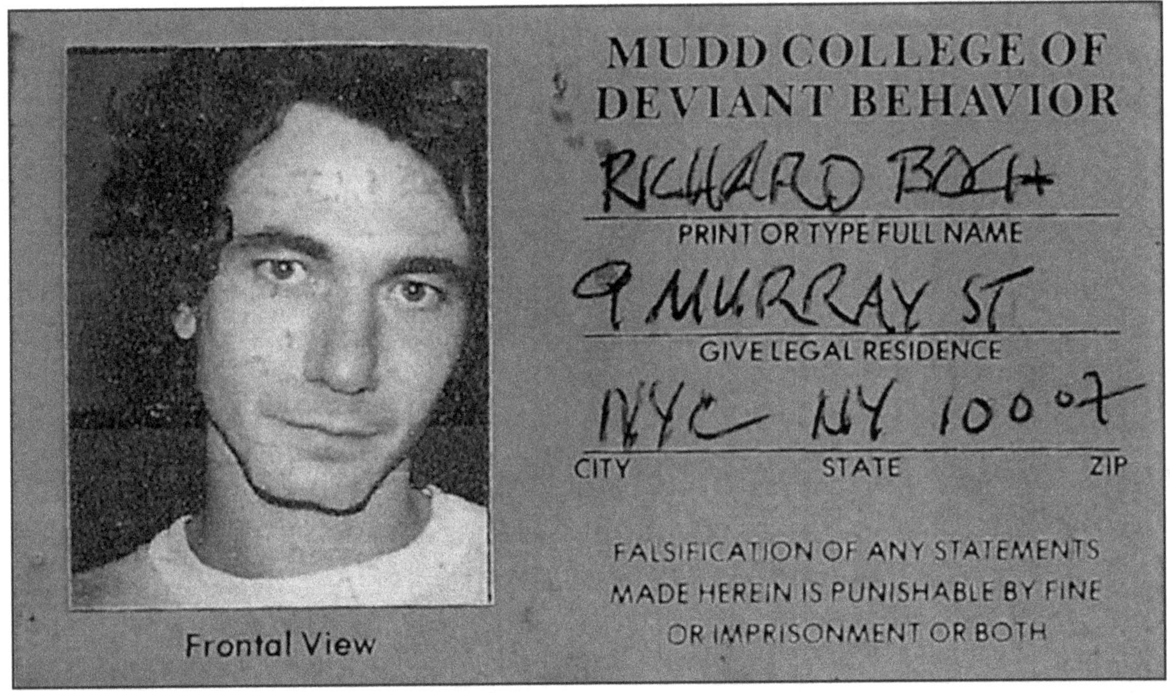

MUDD COLLEGE OF DEVIANT BEHAVIOR

RICHARD BOCH

PRINT OR TYPE FULL NAME

9 MURRAY ST

GIVE LEGAL RESIDENCE

NYC NY 10007

CITY STATE ZIP

FALSIFICATION OF ANY STATEMENTS MADE HEREIN IS PUNISHABLE BY FINE OR IMPRISONMENT OR BOTH

Frontal View

The “B52s” invited me to Max’s Kansas City to see this new New Wave artist, Klaus Nomi. That was the night I met Steve Mass. Steve told me that he was going to open a new night club with Diego Cortez and Anya Phillips. He said that there was going to be a roll down garage door in front of the stage, so if he didn’t like the band, he could just roll down the door. He told me that the “B52s” were going to be the debut act at the club and that I was invited to visit the club anytime. The only time I ever had any trouble getting in the Mudd Club was the one time Keith Haring was the doorman.

Keith’s Mudd College of Deviant Behavior card,I found on the internet. Mr. Boch sent me his.

Dana Downs, Teresa Blair and Vic Varney with a box of my posters that I was now trying to sell for 52¢ or two for a dollar.

This is the self-commissioned poster I made for the “”B52s”” and this image became their first album cover designed by Sue Absurd.

Debi Mazar, gatekeeper at the Mudd College of Deviant Behavior. One night, Keith Haring was the doorman and wouldn't let me in until I threatened to call Steve Mass, the owner.

This has to be Halloween 1978 when the "B52s" were the first band to play the Mudd College of Deviant Behavior.
They played three nights.

The "B52s" onstage at the Mudd College of Deviant Behavior.
Dressed for Halloween.

The "B52s" really packed the house.

This lady is Phyllis Stapler. She was pals with the “B52s”
Here she is in the basement of the Mudd College of Deviant Behavior.

Phyllis Stapler and her rubber ducky pushing Glenn O'Brien aside.

Phyllis Stapler got on stage. I didn't know her rubber duck could sing.

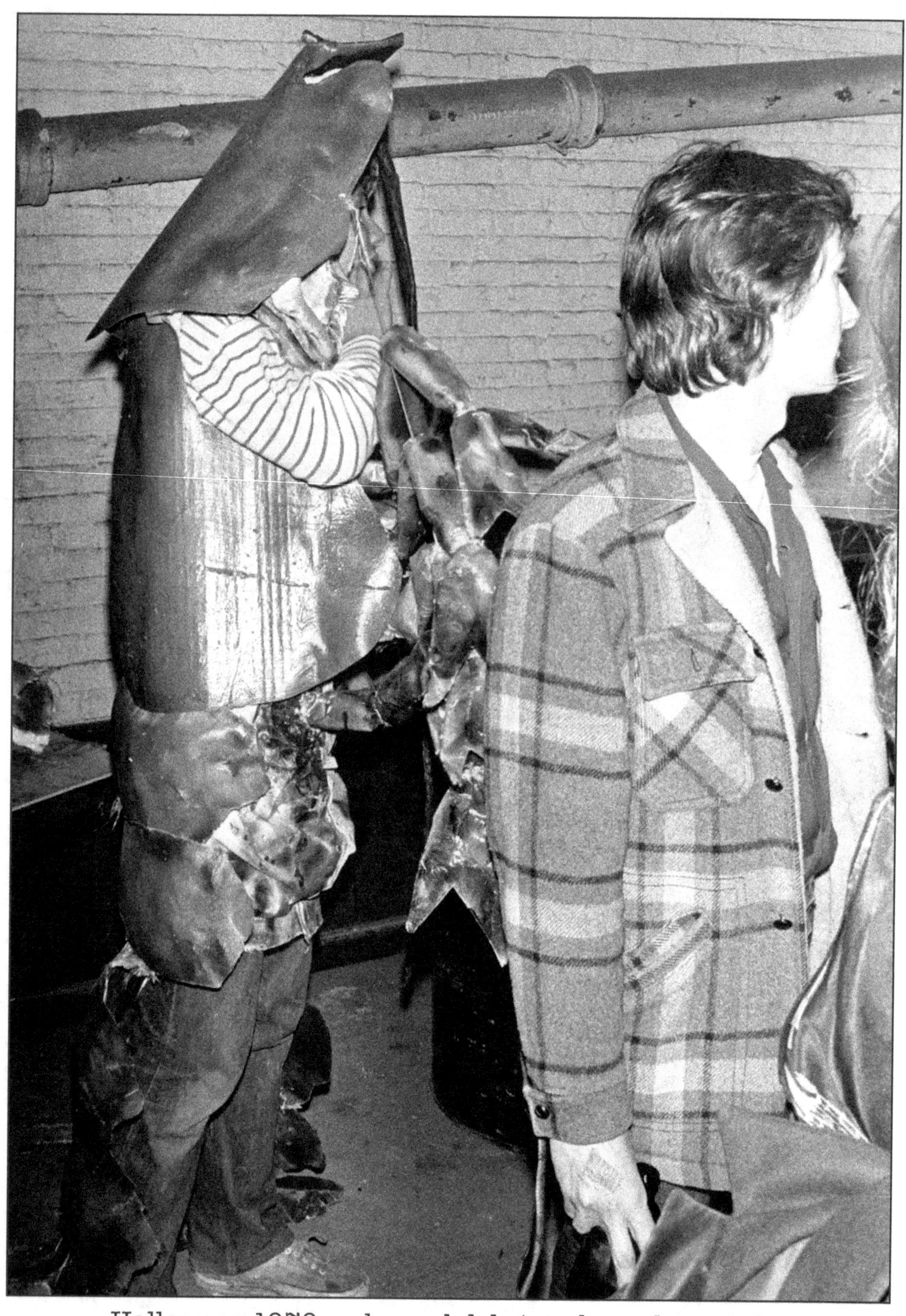

Halloween 1978 and a rock lobster showed up at the Mudd College of Deviant Behavior.

Here is better look at this fantastic rock lobster.
"Rock Lobster" being the "B52s" first hit.

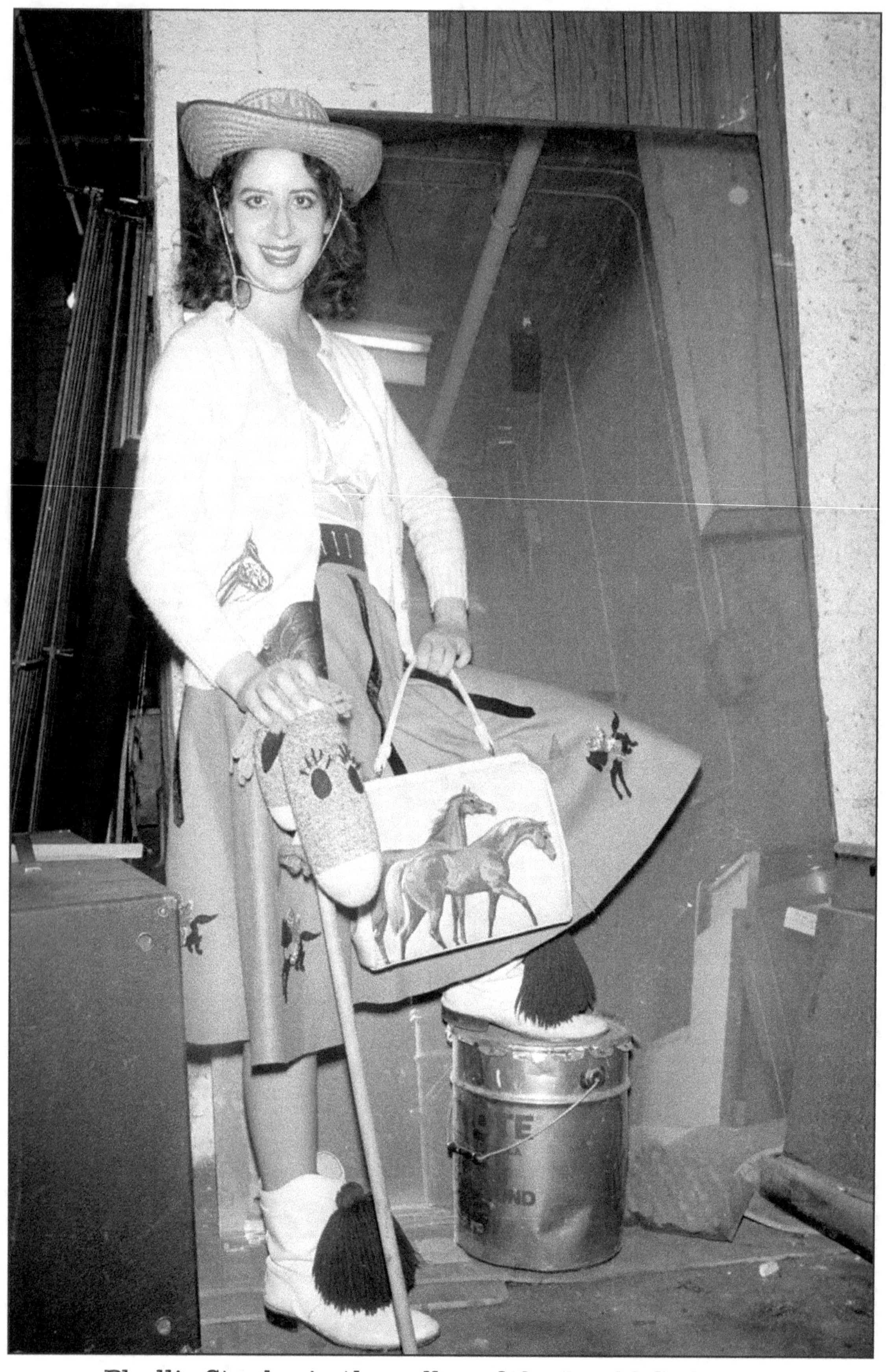

Phyllis Stapler in the cellar of the Mudd College of Deviant Behavior when the "B52s" opened the club.

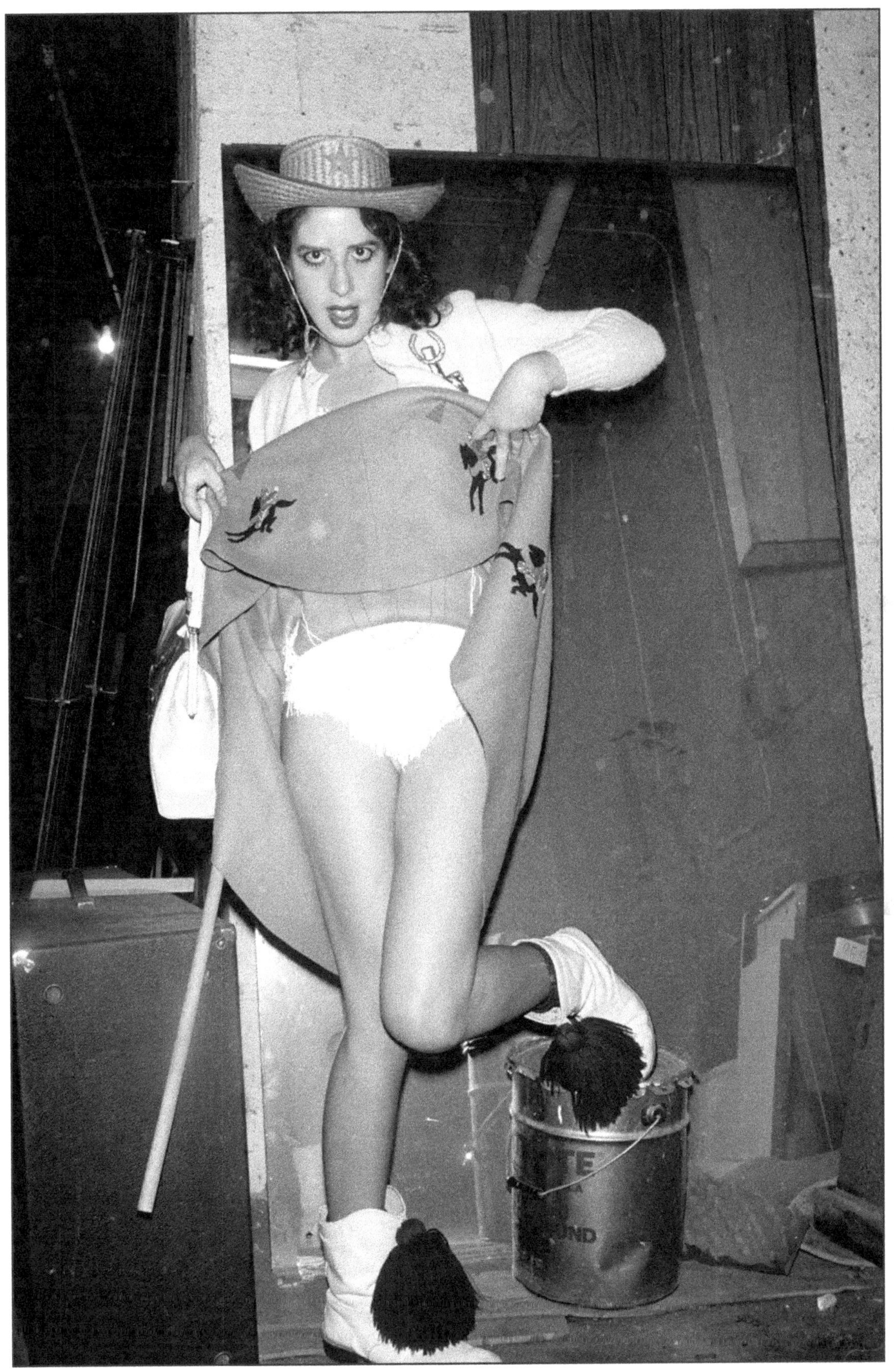

Here's Ms. Stapler showing off.
I didn't ask her to do this.

Kate Pierson of the "B52s" celebrating Halloween
at the Mudd College of Deviant Behavior.

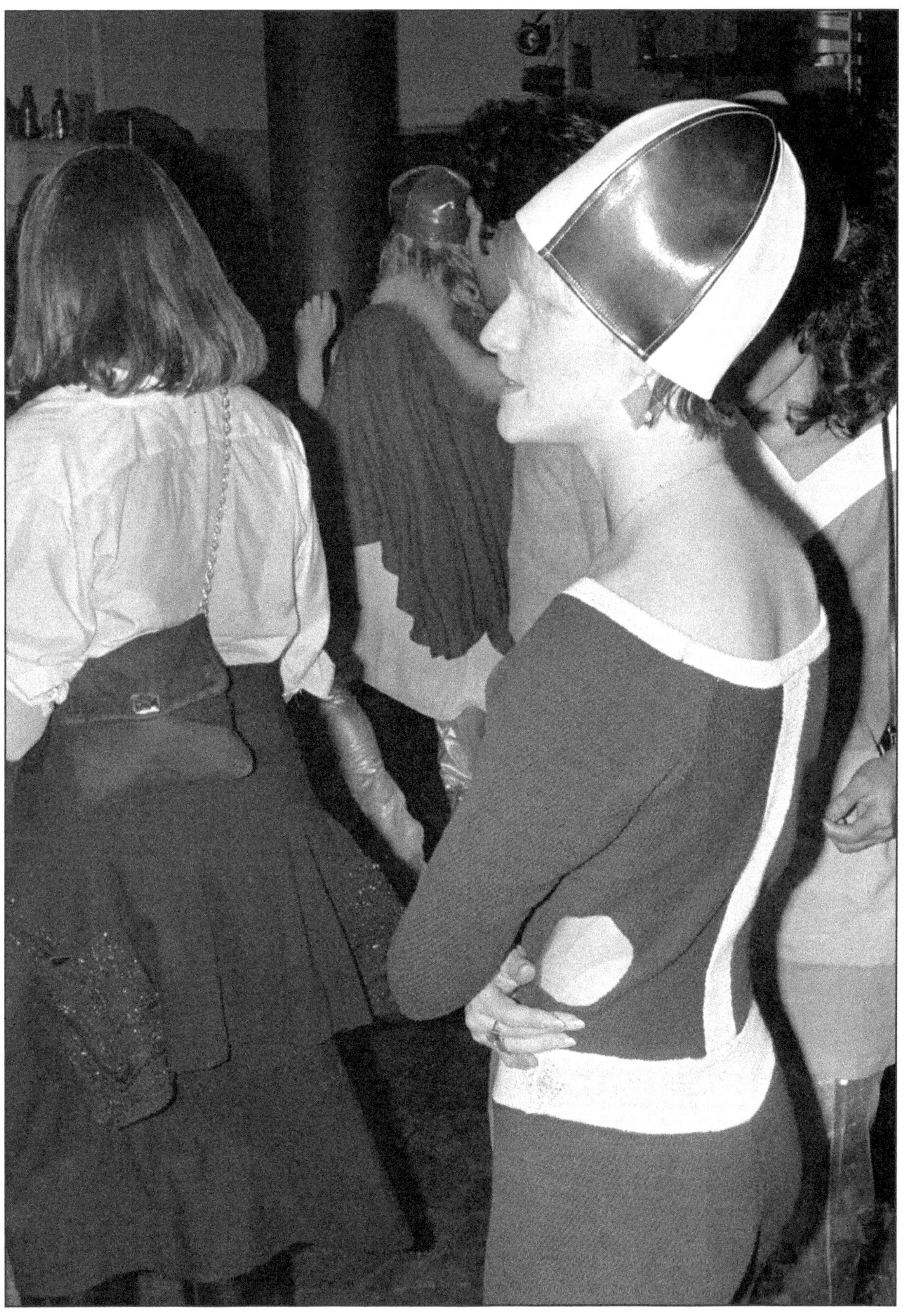

Tekla Turrell at the "B52s" show at the
Mudd College of Deviant Behavior.

Is this Molly Parson, an English fashion designer?

New York Times' street fashion photographer, Bill Cunningham here at the first fashion show at the Mudd College of Deviant Behavior.

Don't know who this lady is, but she got around.
You will see another photo of her later at Danceteria.

Janet Tuckerman, stylist, Hans Pelgrom, Dutch photographer, ?
and Dorian Lipman, stylist.

Another shot of Bill Cunningham, who kept getting in front of my camera blocking my shots. He was nice about it however.

Fashion models at the Mudd College of Deviant Behavior's first fashion show.

Fashion at the Mudd Club often went to extremes.

Kate Simon, photographer second from the right.

Ming Vauze aka Benjamin Liu.
Looking fantastic.

Fred Schneider playing at their
Mudd College of Deviant Behavior gig on Halloween 1978.

Fred Schneider, Tekla Turrell and party people at the Mudd College of Deviant Behavior on Halloween 1978.

Don't spill it, Fred.
Mudd College of Deviant Behavior opening nights.

Assault with a hand bag. Fred Schneider and Tekla Turrell
at the Mudd College of Deviant Behavior.

In the cellar of the Mudd College of Deviant Behavior. Cindy Wilson, author in the mirror, Kate Pierson and Barbara Colaciello in the mirror. Opening nights at the Mudd College of Deviant Behavior.

L>R: Steve Mass, Mudd Club owner, William Burroughs, John Giorno, ?, Fred Schneider, and James Grauerholz in the Mudd College of Deviant Behavior's basement.

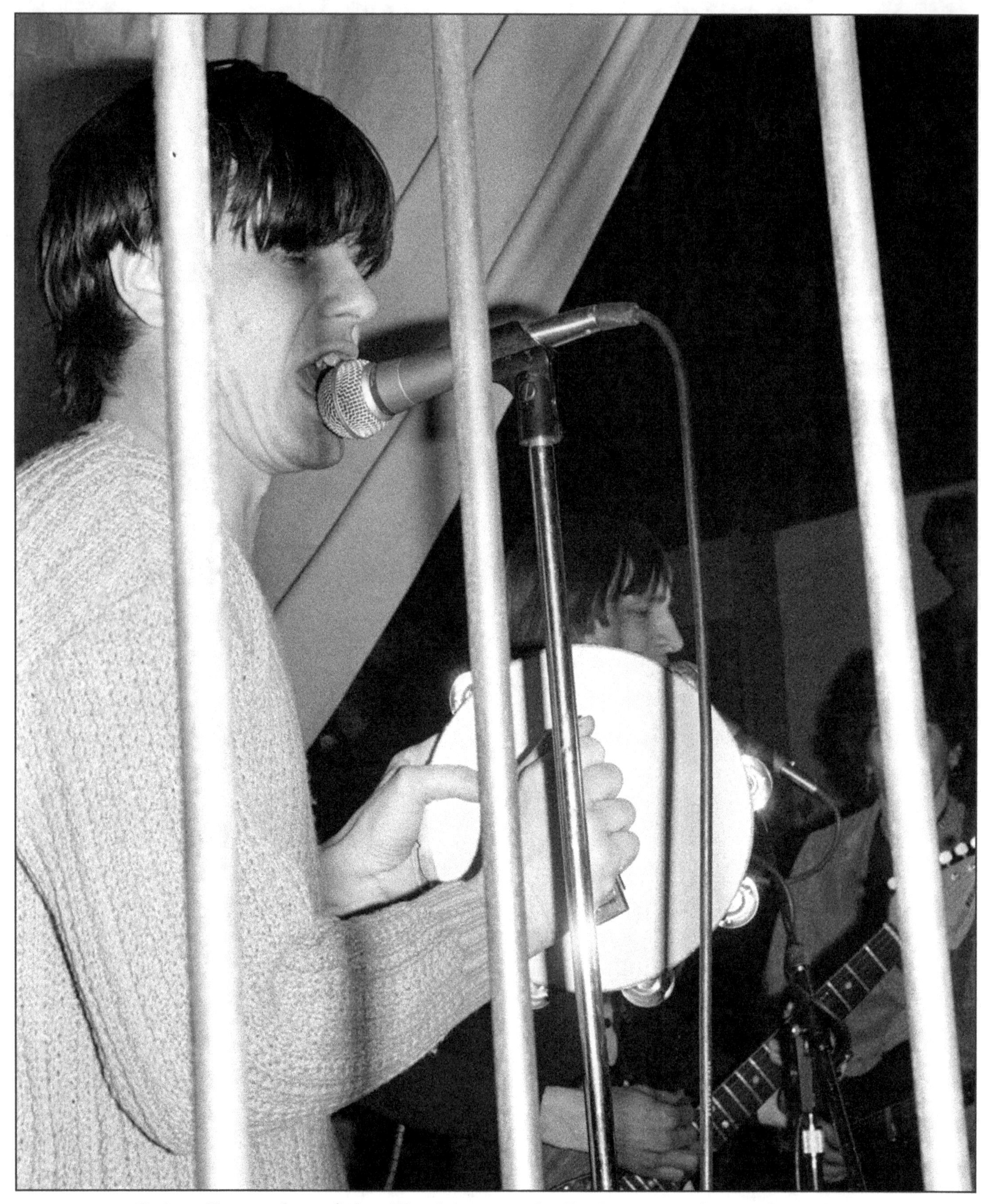

Peter Zaremba of the Fleshtones. Still playing after 50 years.

Debbie Harry playing trumpet at the Red Star Records benefit at the Mudd College of Deviant Behavior.

Fleshtones at the Mudd College of Deviant Behavior. One of the first bands to play after the “B52s” played the opening nights.

Peter Zaremba and Keith Strang of the Fleshtones at the Red Star Records benefit at the Mudd College of Deviant Behavior.

Chaos at the Mudd College of Deviant Behavior.

Walter Steding performing at the Red Star Records benefit at the Mudd College of Deviant Behavior.

Ruby St.Catherine, the bass player for
Walter Steding's band "The Dragon People".

Ronnie Cutrone designed these cages for the Mudd College of Deviant Behavior's GoGo dancers.

L>R: Lenny Ferraro, Ruby, Walter's bassist, Walter Steding and Chris Stein in Ronnie Cutrone's cage at the Mudd College of Deviant Behavior.

Ronnie Cutrone at the Mudd College of Deviant Behavior.

Linny Morris
One of the beauties at the William Coupon exhibit at the Mudd College of Deviant Behavior.

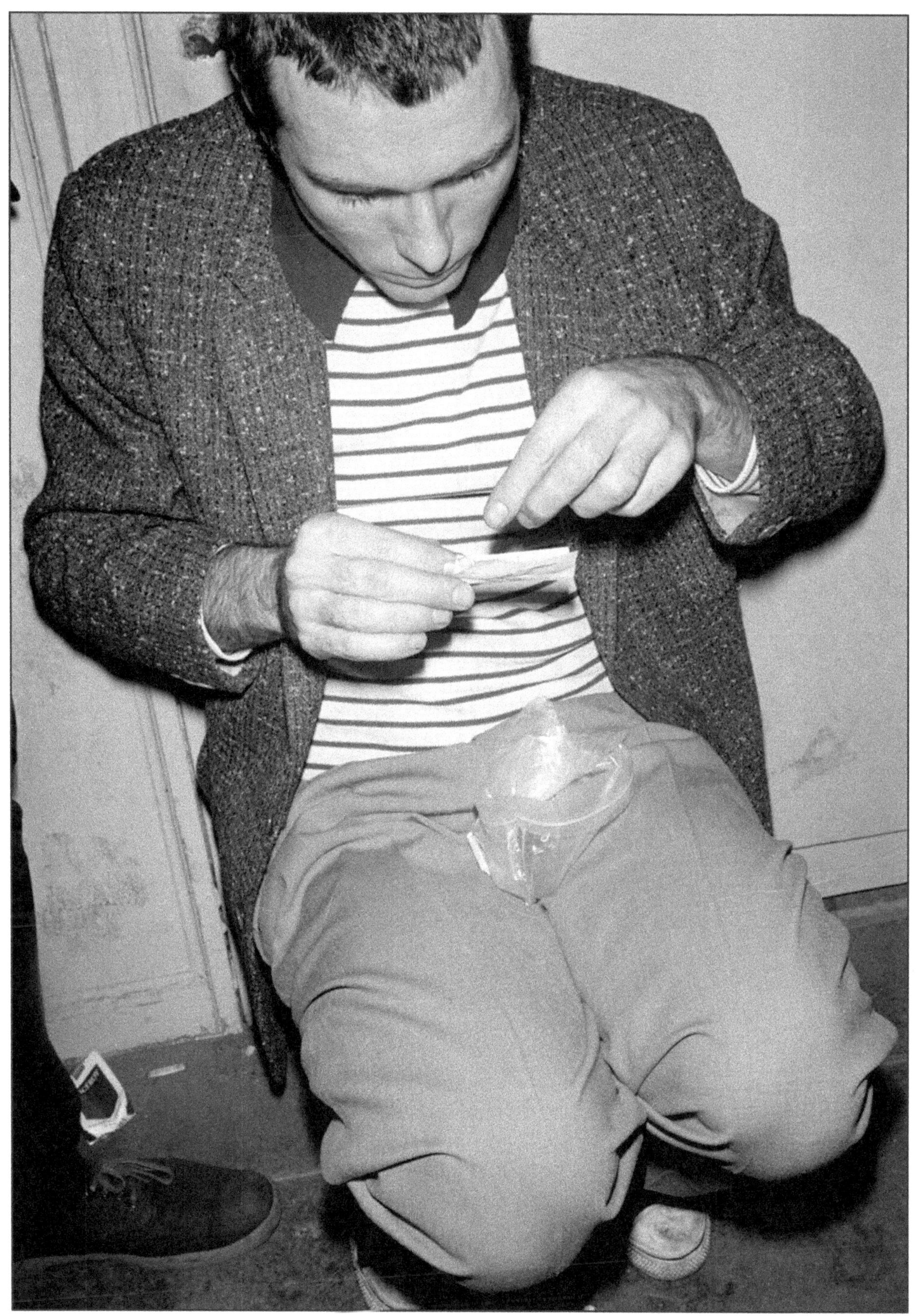

On the opening night of the Mudd College of Deviant Behavior, I saw Glenn O'Brien rolling a joint. I saw him later at a party cleaning his seeds on the coffee table. I said, "Can't you do that at home?" He said, "I smoke more marijuana than any white man on earth."

Glenn O'Brien, here as the MC of the Red Star Records benefit at the Mudd College of Deviant Behavior.

Frank Zappa and David Azarch spinning at the Mudd College of Deviant Behavior.

Sara Driver, movie director and Richard Cramer, assistant art director for "Interview".

? and David Azarch, Mudd College of Deviant Behavior's regular DJ.

Legs McNeil, writer and Teresa Blair at the Mudd College of Deviant Behavior.

On the right, Teresa and one of the musicians in the band that Legs McNeil managed, “Shrapnel”.

Alan Tannenbaum, photographer, at the Mudd College of Deviant Behavior.

Don't remember this girl's name, but she got into all the clubs. You can see my original poster for the "B52s" up on the column to the right.

David Bowie at the Mudd College of Deviant Behavior.

Wendy Whitlaw, stylist and ? at the Mudd College of Deviant Behavior.

Tiny Tim waiting to get in to the Mudd College of Deviant Behavior.

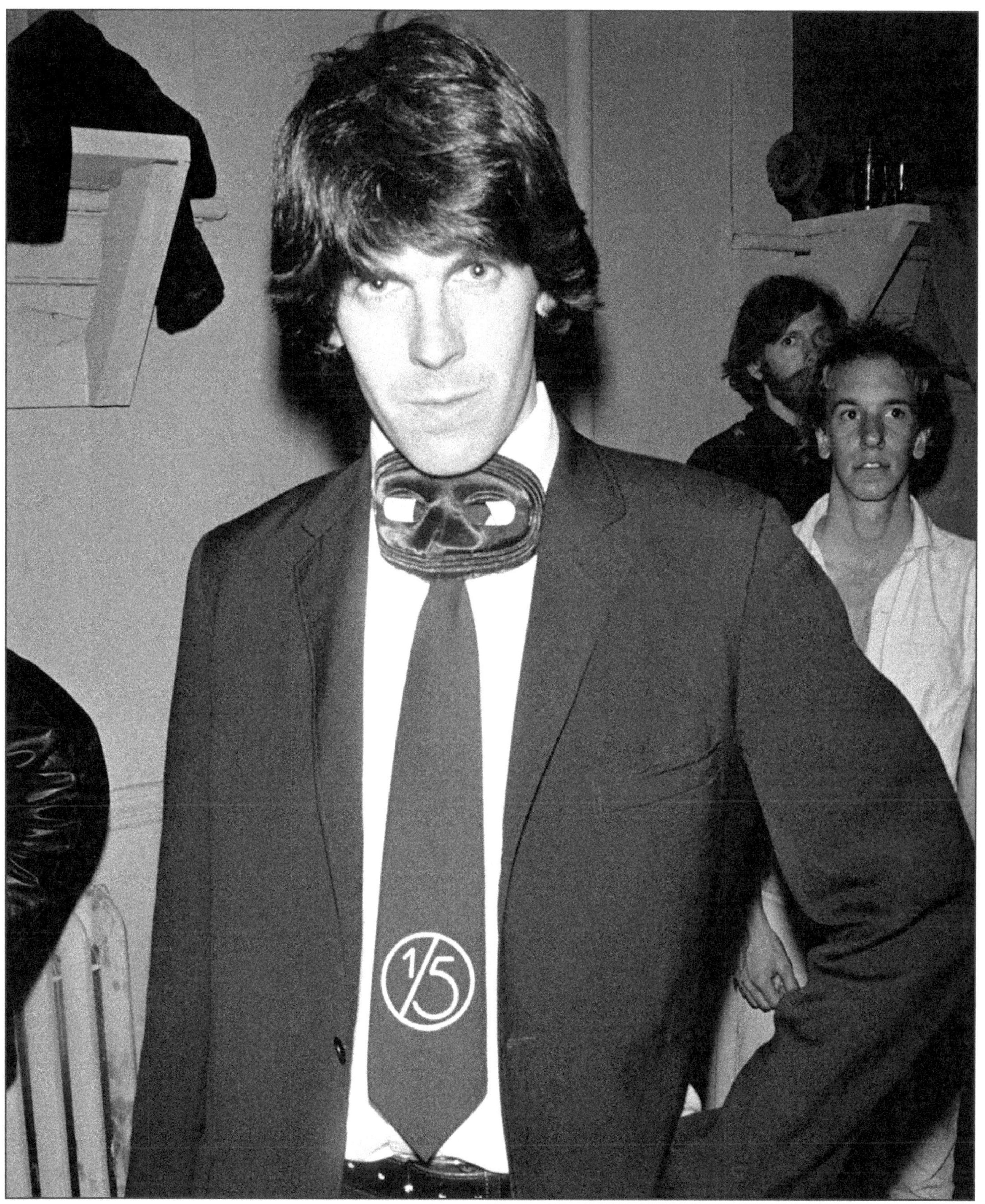

Robert Waldrop wrote lyrics for the "B52s".
I think the song was "Dirty Back Roads".

John Rhodes, reporter and Dorian Lipman, stylist at the "B52s'" first shows at the Mudd College of Deviant Behavior.

Lisa Stroud and Tina L'Hotsky.

Tina L'Hotsky, self-proclaimed Queen of the
Mudd College of Deviant Behavior.
She was a poet, actress and film maker.

Mudd College of Deviant Behavior regulars.

Jackie Shapiro with a William Coupon exhibit at the Mudd College of Deviant Behavior.

Mudd College of Deviant Behavior regulars

Curtis Knapp, photographer and Teresa Blair at the Mudd College of Deviant Behavior.

Glenn O'Brien, Amos Poe, filmmaker and Fab Five Freddy Mudd College of Deviant Behavior.

Richard Reinhardt and Annette Sbarro. She made him quit the Ramones.

Michael Musto. writer, surrounded by fans at the Mudd Club.

Steve Mass, the Mudd College of Deviant Behavior's owner told me that Princess Stephanie of Monaco was in the house and he wanted a picture. As who I thought was the princess had bodyguards, I had to sneak this photo of someone dancing with Betsy Johnson, the fashion designer.
It was a one shot "hope and poke" and then I danced away.
My wife and others now tell me that isn't Ms. Monaco.

Oy! The fog of war.

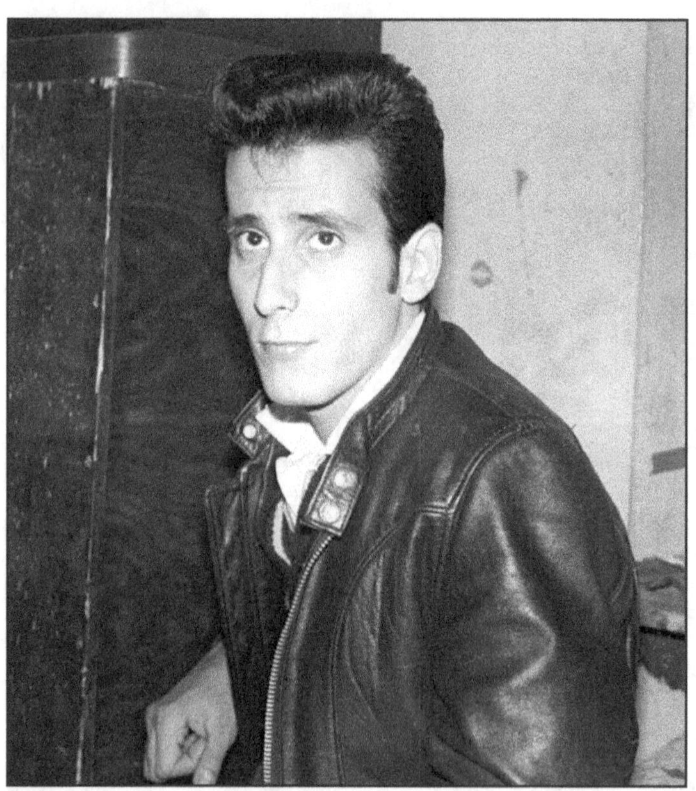

Nice retro hairstyle.

Yejong Son and Sally Randall Brugen at the Mudd College of Deviant Behavior

Brad Balfour at the Mudd College of Deviant Behavior.

Dana Downs, one of the earliest "B52s" fans.

Sally Randall Brugen, working a door somewhere.

Teresa Blair, ex-Little Miss Sunbeam bread and Dana Downs in front of the door to the Mudd College of Deviant Behavior.

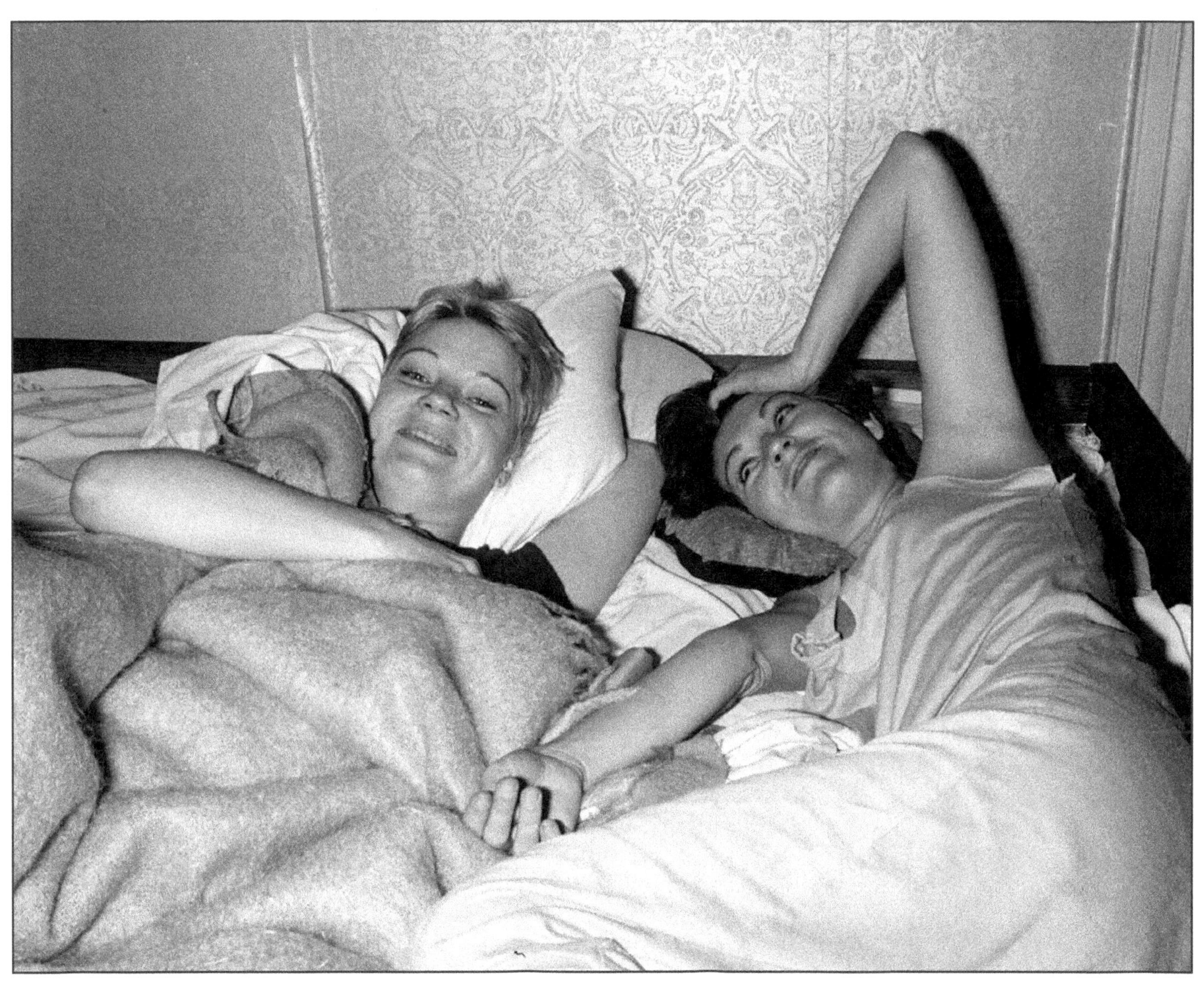

Teresa and Dana recovering.
Teresa and Dana were original fans of the “B52s” from Athens, GA.

"Was, Not Was" at the Mudd Club.

Joe Jackson's first gig in the US was at the
Mudd College of Deviant Behavior.
Is she really going out with him?

Steve Mass, the boss at the Mudd College of Deviant Behavior.
When REM played the Mudd College of Deviant Behavior,
he didn't want to pay them.
They went on and played for free in front of 12 people.

Marianne Faithfull at the Mudd College of Deviant Behavior
at 0230.
Some of us had to work the next day.

STUDIO 54

When I first moved to New Jersey in 1975, disco music was really popular and if one was trying to meet girls, dancing in discos was a good way to start. I would visit the Soap Factory, a huge disco in Palisades Park, NJ.

I also went to Le Jardin, a Manhattan disco at the Diplomat Hotel's basement, where there were better DJs. I remember hearing a remix of the Temptations "Standing On Shaky Ground" that seemed to play forever.

But being a rocker at heart with my musical roots starting with the British invasion of the '60s, I would also venture from New Jersey to Manhattan looking for clubs that played rock music. There was Great Gildersleeves, but that club seemed to feature mostly unknown heavy metal bands.

Someone told me I should check out a club in Manhattan's East Village called CBGBs. I found CB's one Saturday night and paid my $3.50 admission. The band was "Television". A punk band featuring Richard Lloyd and Tom Verlaine. It didn't take me very long watching the two guitarists to think to myself, why are these guys playing so poorly. I had taken guitar lessons as a teenager, hadn't touched a guitar in 10 years, but I thought I could play better than those two on stage. I went back to the doorperson and asked for my money back. Didn't get it.

When the "B52s" invited me to come to Max's Kansas City to see a New Wave artist, Klaus Nomi, they were with a guy named Steve Mass. Steve told me he was opening a rock club on Halloween 1978 and the "B52s" were the opening act. The Mudd College of Deviant Behavior was to become "my" club where one would hear the newest of the New Wave.

When Studio 54 opened, I thought it was just another disco. When my pals at "Interview" magazine invited me and put me on the guest list, I was surprised at the massive dance floor, balconies all the way to the roof, fabulous lighting and a superior sound system. It was quite impressive.

However, when I went to Studio 54 and was not on any guest list, I often wouldn't be allowed past the doorman. I remember I once went wearing white pants, white shirt and white Capizio dance shoes. I knew the doorman, but when Haoui Montaug ignored me, I said, "Hey Haoui, are you going to let me in?"

"No, you look like an ice cream man!"

The next week they had a party for Barry White and one had to wear white.

I didn't go...

Haoui Montaug, one of Studio 54's doormen and Steve Rubell, one of the disco's owners. Now Haoui is wearing white, but somehow doesn't look like an ice cream man.

Haoui Montaug, was a doorman at several clubs besides Studio 54. He always gave me a hard time getting any club where he was working the door...

Aleph Ashline and Steven Saben.
Aleph was one of Studio 54's doormen.

Jim Fouratt, one of the organizers of Danceteria.

Maripol, a fashion designer and stylist and
Christina Moser the singer
of the duo “Krisma” with Maurizio Arcieri.

Michael Musto, a magazine writer, who got around a lot.

Glenn O'Brien.

Richard Johnson, newspaper reporter and sailor.

David Johansen aka Buster Poindexter at Studio 54.
David was always “camera friendly”.

Rockets Redglare, I think he was a comedian.

Joey Arias, Klaus Nomi's pal.

One of the characters who lit up the night at Studio 54.

Coati Mundi aka Andy Hernandez of Kid Creole fame and Glenn O'Brien.

Marc Balet, the art director of "Interview" magazine.

I used to go with the A&M Records promotion director and various artists to visit the local radio stations. When Bryan Adams released his first single "Let Me Take You Dancing", I asked the A&M promotion guy, "Where is the party for Bryan tonight?" When I learned that no party was planned for Bryan, I called my gal pal at "Interview" and asked her if we could all go to Studio 54 and try to get the DJ to play Bryan's new single. L>R, Barbara Colaciello, the WKTU program director, Bryan, Rupert Smith who made a lot of Warhol's paintings and a friend of Barbara's.

Bryan Adams and the WKTU program director in the DJ booth at Studio 54. Bryan got his disco hit played.

Barbara, Bryan and ?.

"Let Me Take You Dancing" was a great disco song.
Bryan told me that it wasn't originally a disco song, but the record producer changed it. Bryan wasn't happy about that.

Who took this photo of Barbara and me?
I look like I am blowing a horn.

Michael Shnayerson, writer for Vanity Fair
and his posse at Studio 54.

Michael Shnayerson taking a break.
Libet Stirling and Ashley DuBose in the background

Rick Nielsen of "Cheap Trick", Robin Zander and Joey Ramone
at Studio 54.

? and Anita Sarko DJ.

Andy scouting for portrait commissions at Studio 54. Andy looks like he doesn't recognize me, but I was processing his films the next day.

Andy, Cornelia Guest, Jon Gould, Keith Haring at Studio 54.

Walter Steding, muscian, Paul Colliton, photographer and Fred Schneider of the "B52s".

Tommy Gunn and Diane Brill. Tommy was an early computer animator who used a mouse upside down like it was a trackball...

Robert Molnar, Fred's pal, Anita Sarko, DJ and Mr. Schneider.

Richard Bernstein, cover artist for “Interview” and
Richard Cramer, assistant art director for “Interview”.

L>R: Rod Stewart. Steve Rubell, Alana Stewart,
Alan Carr at Studio 54.

L>R: Alana Stewart. Alan Carr and Rod Stewart at Studio 54.

Steve Rubell, principal of Studio 54 and
Lisa Robinson, talent scout and writer.

Aleph Ashline, doorman and Steven Saban, writer.

DANCETERIA

Another nightclub in Manhattan that was popular with the New Wave crowd.

A multi-level club with a stage for live performance and a roof where there was a BBQ and live performances in the summer.

Rudolf Piper and Jim Fouratt were the principals.

It is written that Danceteria was Madonna's first performance, but that isn't true. I photographed Ms. M at Uncle Sam's Blues, a biker bar in Roslyn, Long Island. I did take a few shots of Madonna on the roof with her brother and another dancer.

Besides booking up and coming bands from the US and Europe, there were occasional art shows.

While there were three different locations for the club in Manhattan, I only visited the 21st Street location and the short-lived Hamptons Danceteria in Watermill, Long Island.

Madonna on the rooftop of Danceteria NY.
Now she had replaced her live musicans and sang to a tape recording.
Here she is with her brother., Christopher and Erika Bell.
I had brought Yuki Watanabe and Michael O'Brien
who were scouting new artists to take to Club NY,
a monthly event at a nightclub in Boston.

Glenn O'Brien and his self-portrait at the Danceteria art exhibit.

Didn't ask for his passport.

Diane Brill and Rudolf Piper.

Rudolf Piper at the Danceteria art exhibit.

Diane Brill at the Danceteria art exhibit. Diane told me that she eats a pound of chocolate daily to keep her voluptous figure.

Yuki Watanabe at the Danceteria art exhibit.

Aleph at the Danceteria art exhibit.

Jean Caffiene, musician and artist at an art exhibit at Danceteria NY.
Jean was also a member of the all-woman band "Pulsellama".
Whose single I did a cover for.

Maripol, fashion designer and Polaroid artist.

Robyn Geddes, artist and Warhol assistant.

Haoui Montaug at the Danceteria art exhibit.

Deanna Anderson, artist at an art exhibit at the Mudd Club
curated by Sally Randall Brugen.

Diane Brill and Rudolf Piper.

Rudolf Piper, Diane Brill and Anita Sarko DJ.

August Darnell aka Kid Creole, Diane Brill and Rudolp Piper at Club Sandwich. Now if I could only remember where Club Sandwich was.

L>R: Alan Rish, Diane Brill and Adriana Kaegi, the lead Coconut in Kid Creole's band.

Rudolf Piper and Christopher Makos (photographer and assistant to Man Ray).

Eric Mitchell, film maker and Christopher Makos, photographer.

gwenl and Thérèse...her real name was Teresa Spelta,
the singers of "Nonpareil" at Danceteria.

David Lichtenstein, performing with "Nonpareil" at Danceteria.

HURRAH'S

Hurrah's was unusual in that it was a discotheque that played the newest videos as well as hosting concerts by up-and-coming artists.

The "B52s" played there, but I wound up being stage security and didn't take any photos that night. Squeeze, Chris Spedding, Pylon, Walter Steding, Richard Strange and Klaus Nomi all performed there.

I will never forget the night that Klaus Nomi invited me to photograph his show at Hurrah's. When I arrived at the entrance, I could see that there was a line around the block of people wanting to get in.

As Klaus said he would put me on the guest list, I skipped the line and went right to the doorman, who happened to be Haoui Montaug. As mentioned earlier, Haoui was gay, I was straight and Haoui liked to give me a hard time gaining entrance to whatever club he happened to be working the door at.

I said, "Klaus put me on the guest list."

"What's your name?", Haoui asked, as if he didn't know.

"George DuBose."

Haoui pretended to scan the guest list and then he said, "He's already in."

One of my friends who knew I was going to Klaus's show used my name to get in.

Klaus Nomi at his performance at Hurrah's. Klaus was just starting to "blow up" and there were 3000 people trying to get in.

Maureen McLaughlin, the first manager of the "B52s".

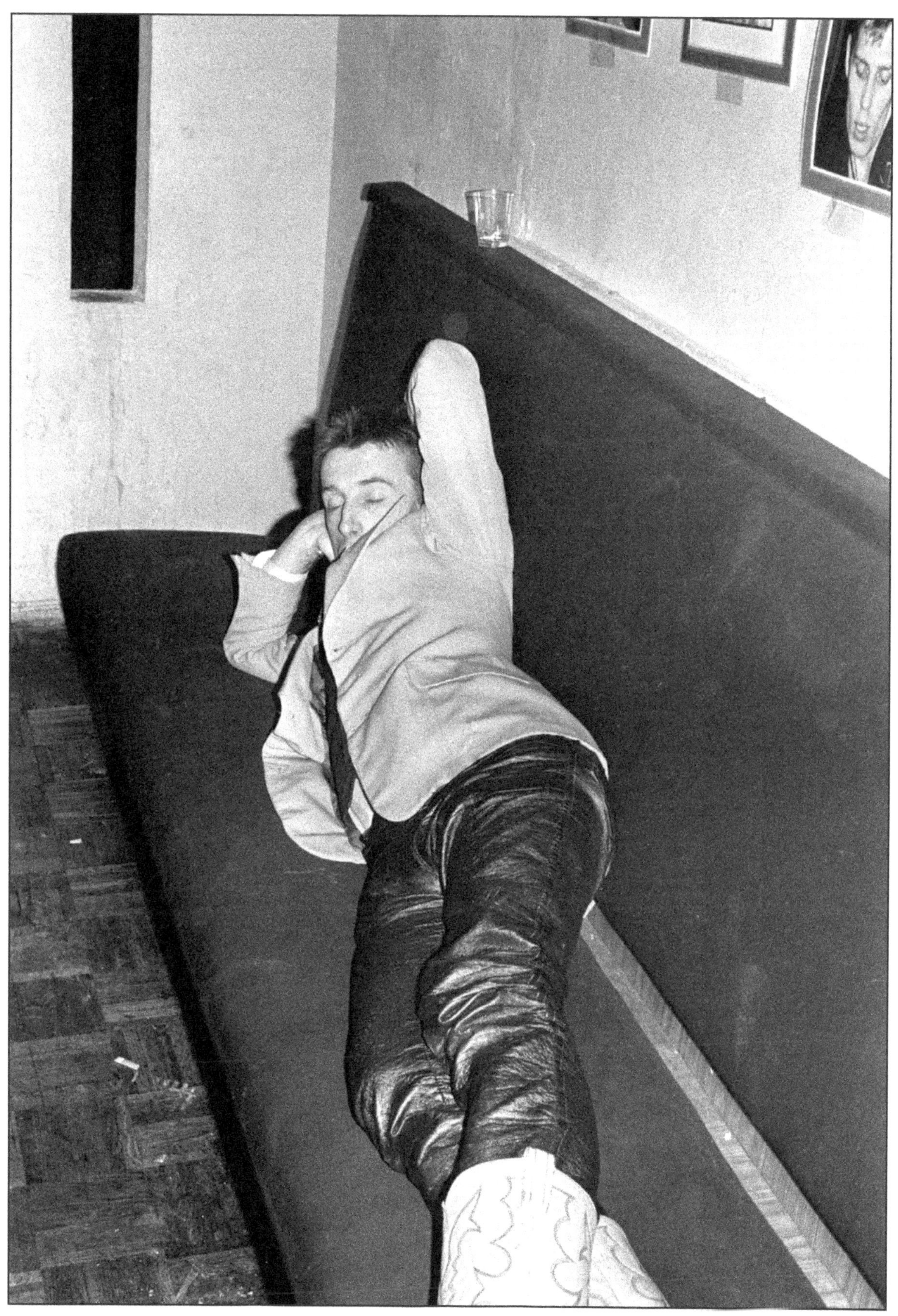

Victor Bokris, author of Warhol's biography,
catching a disco nap at Hurrah's NYC.

Glenn O'Brien's "TV Party" on location at Hurrah's.
L>R: ?, Chris Stein, David Byrne, Kate Simon, ?, Maureen McLaughlin, Eric Mitchel and Glenn.

Edo Bertoglio and Bobby Grossman photographing Kate and Cindy of the "B52s" at their concert at Hurrah's NYC.

Fred Schneider and Joey Aries
at Hurrah's

Fred is the leadsinger of the "B52s" and Joey was Klaus Nomi's pal.

Joey was always dramatic and had many characters.

Looks like Fred is beating Joey with a microphone?

Rick Okasik, of the Cars and friend at the “B52’s concert at Hurrah’s NYC.
Don’t know the zombie on the left.

Sara Driver and friend at the “B52’s” concert at Hurrah’s NYC.

I forget this lady's name, but she was out and about often.

Edwidge and Edo Bertoglio, photographer at Hurrah's.

Richard Strange (UK) sang with his music on a reel to reel tape recorder. He had an LP released on ZE Records for which I did the cover.

Richard Strange on stage at Hurrah's NYC.

Walter Steding and Ruby St.Catherine on stage at Hurrah's NYC.
Walter played his violin through a biofeedback generator and
his boywatcher glasses had blinking lights.

L>R: cameraman, Walter Steding, Glenn O'Brien (don't know what Glenn is doing here) and David Byrne on the keyboard.

DANCETERIA HAMPTONS
WATERMILL

One summer, Danceteria opened a branch office in the Hamptons, specifically Watermill, Long Island. It was conveniently located across the highway from the Green Thumb farm market of Bayview Farms owned by the Halsey family since the 1600s.

I was good friends with the Halsey family and spent many summers picking and grilling sweet corn with my friend, Billy Halsey.

There are many artists living in the Hamptons and this Danceteria was a nice party location.

Here are some photos of an art exhibition that took place there.

Ronnie Cutrone, one of Warhol's assistants
and a great artist on his own.

The author wearing a Halsey farm cap and
Jackie Shapiro, fashion designer at the Danceteria Watermill NY.

Diane Brill and Alan Rish at the Danceteria Watermill NY.

David Whelan aka Joe Hampton, was the leader of the first punk band to come out of the Hamptons.

William Falkenberg, the artist who designed the famous "Fabulous Hamptons" t-shirt.

Robert Chapman, one of the most talented artists I know.
He was also an assistant to Willem de Kooning.
Robert's work ranges from abstract seen here to photorealism.

Beauty just "hanging out" at the Danceteria in Watermill, NY.

Kieran Murphy, being a DJ.

L>R: Matt Whelan, guitarist, Joe Hampton, singer, Paul Colliton at the Danceteria Watermill, NY.

Paul Colliton and ?. Paul is wearing the famous "Fabulous Hamptons" t-shirt designed by Bill Falkenberg, artist.

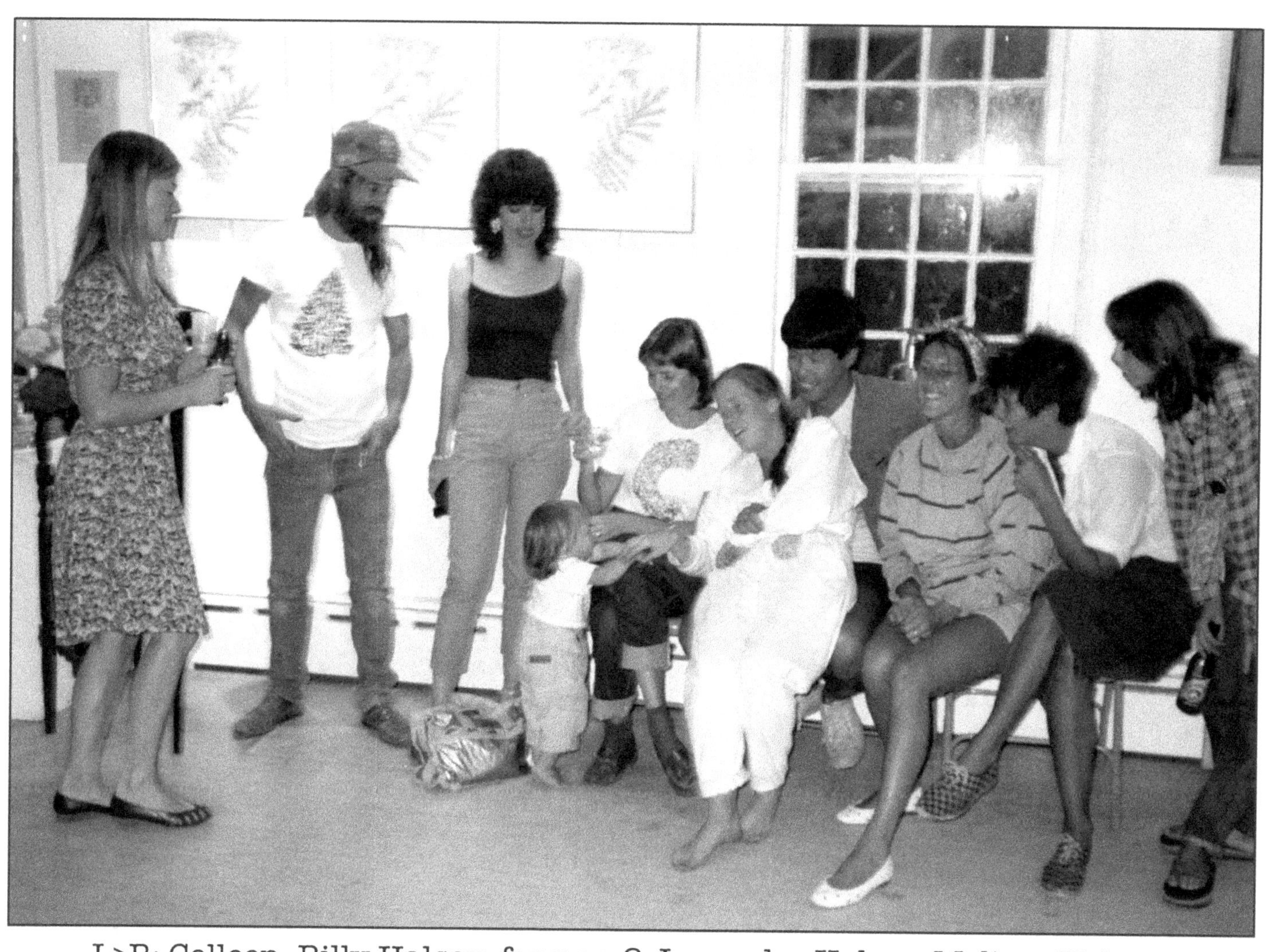

L>R: Colleen, Billy Halsey, farmer, ?, Lavender Halsey, Melissa Halsey, Ashley DuBose, Yuki Watanabe, Jackie Colliton, Maruka and Shelagh Murphy, artist and assistant to Roy Lichtenstein at the Danceteria Watermill, NY.

Cati, a Belgian princess and Edwidge.
I think this was at the Danceteria in Watermill, NY.

Edwidge as barkeeper.
Remember the daze when one could smoke tobacco in the clubs?

Shelagh Murphy, artist and Carlos Ramos, artist.
Both were assistants to Roy Lichtenstein.

Carlos Ramos is a sculptor and sailor.
On the beach in Bridgehampton, NY.

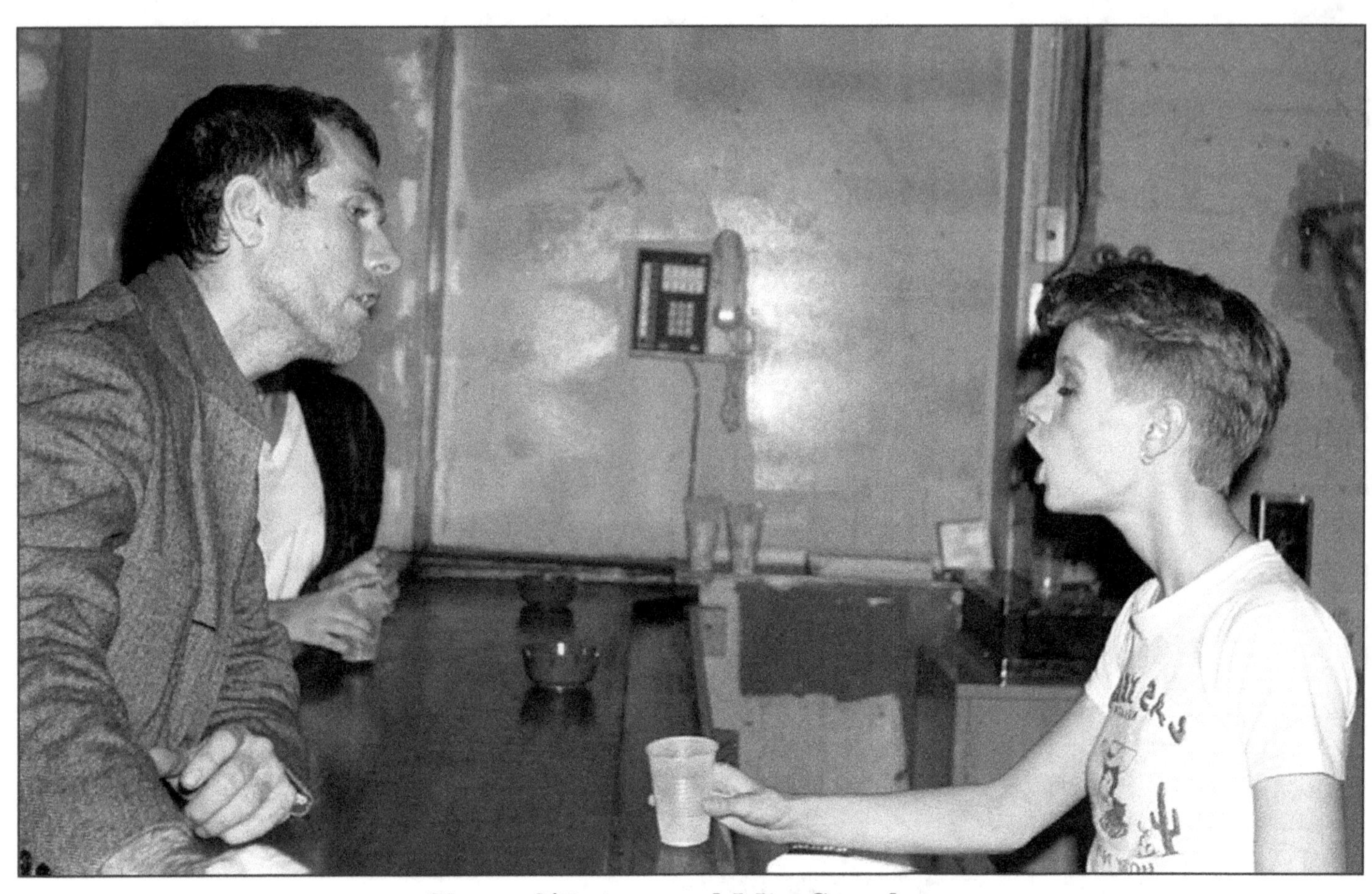

Glenn O'Brien and Min Sanchez.
I think Glenn is looking for a complimentary cocktail.

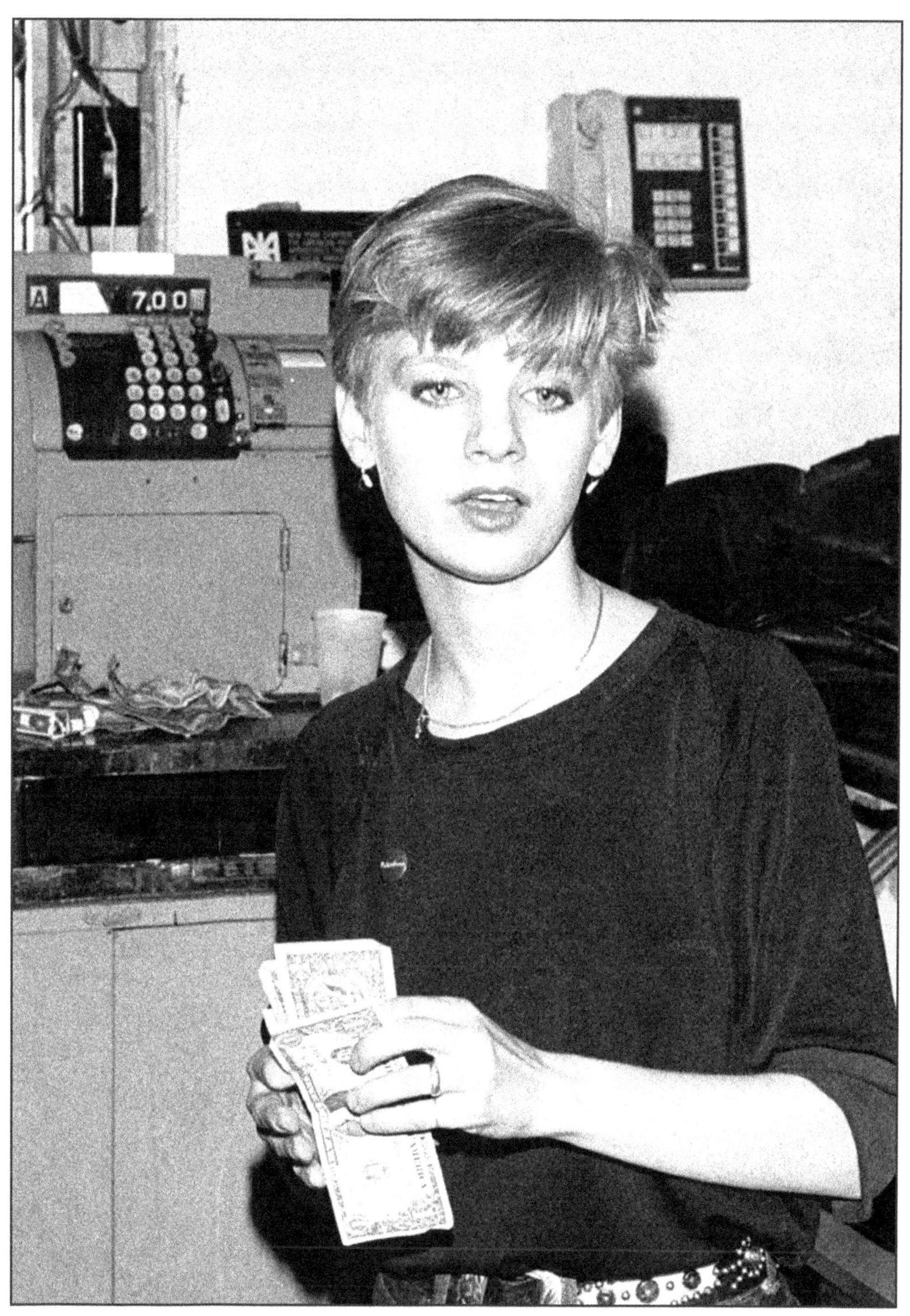

Min Sanchez, the barkeeper rolling the dough.

Min as barkeeper.

The author and Johanna Halsey
have the same birthday, August 13th.

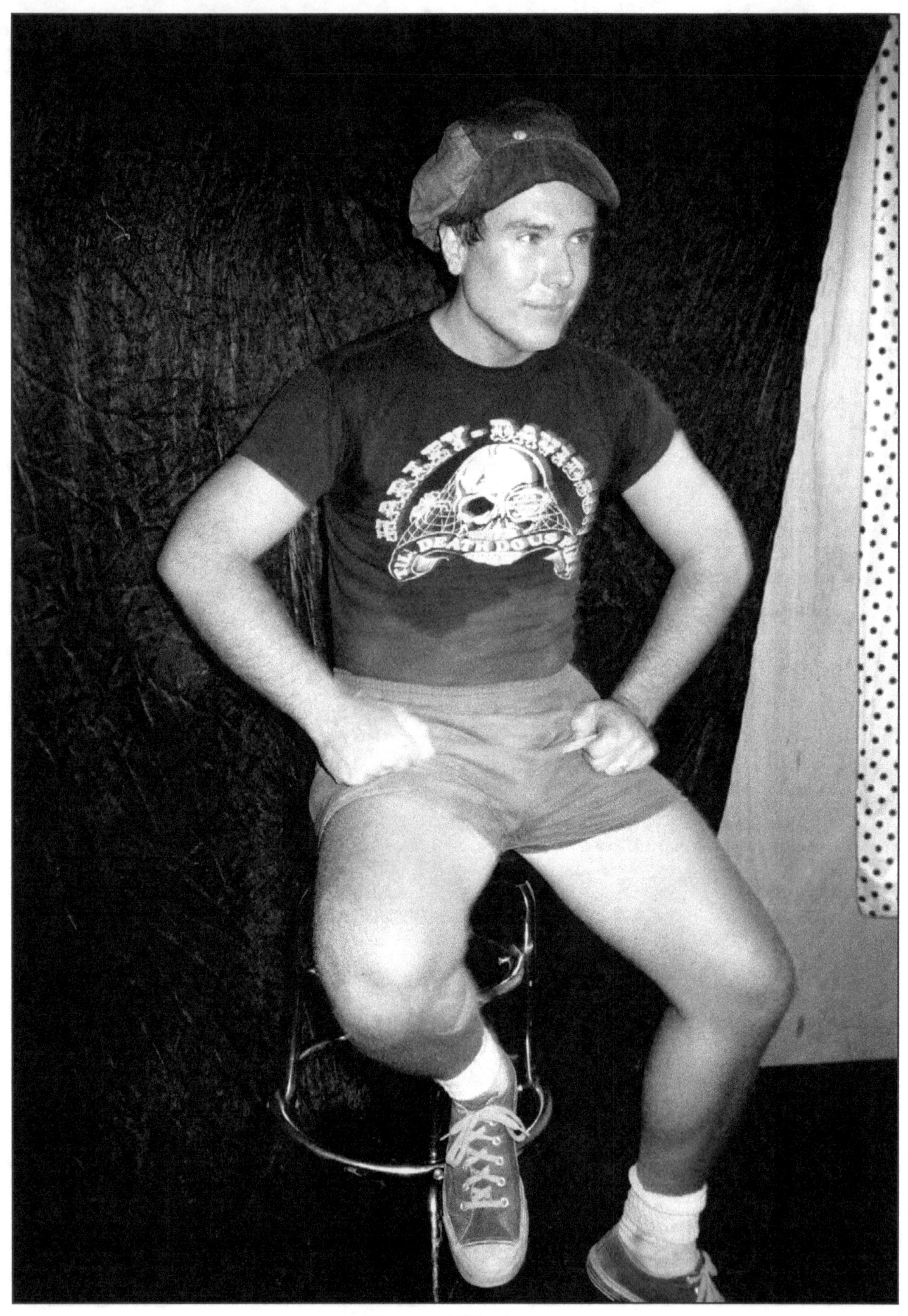

Glenn O’Brien.

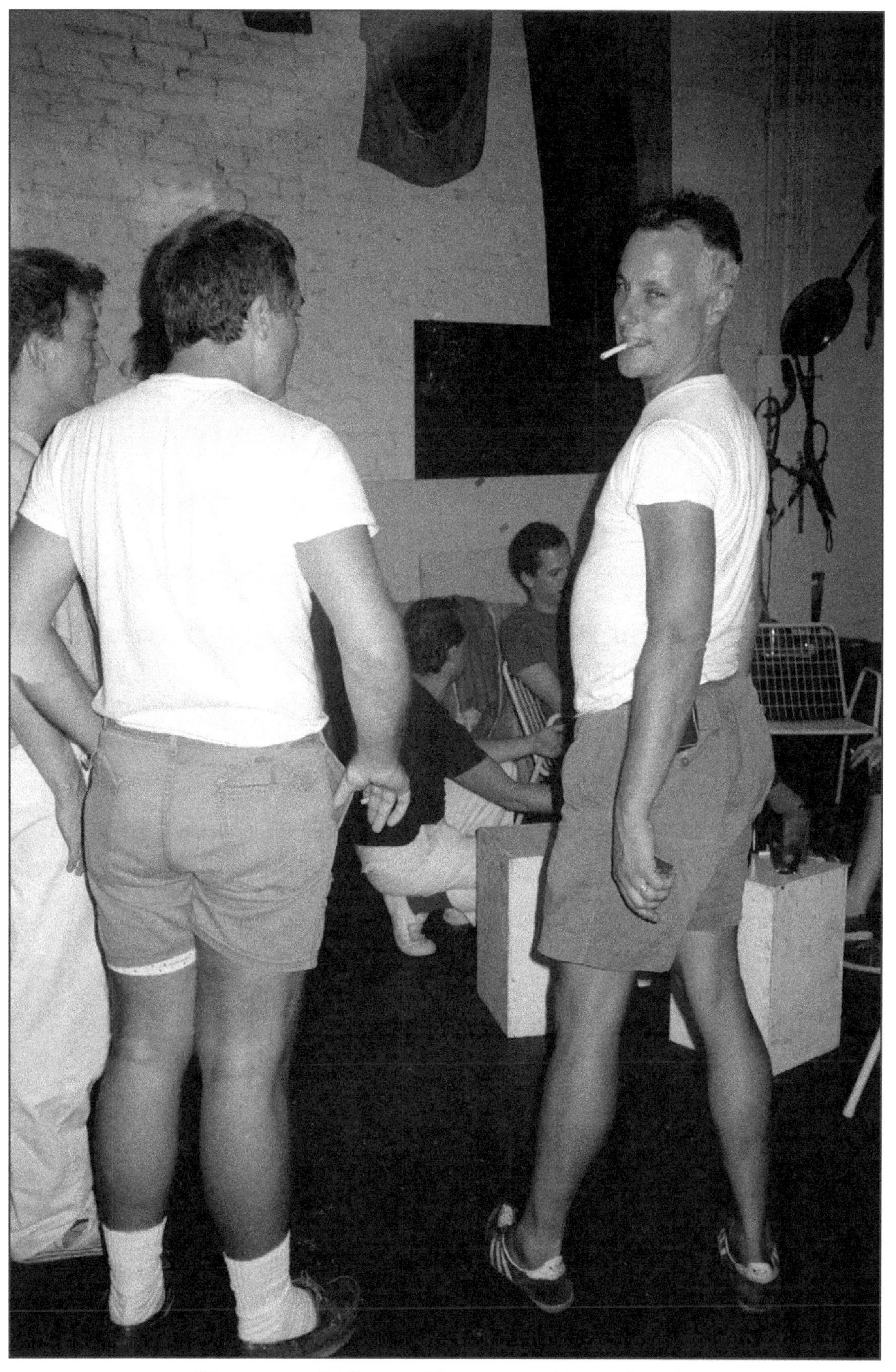

Glenn and the author sporting shorts
Glenn should wear longer shorts or raise his boxers...

THE FOG OF PARTIES

Every weekend, we were either personally invited to parties in Manhattan lofts, apartments or on occasion we would just be walking around Lower Manhattan or the East Side and would hear loud music emenating from the upper floors of an apartment or loft building.

Sometimes we would see a line of people going into a building and we would follow them.

In most cases, we would either know the host or other people at the party.

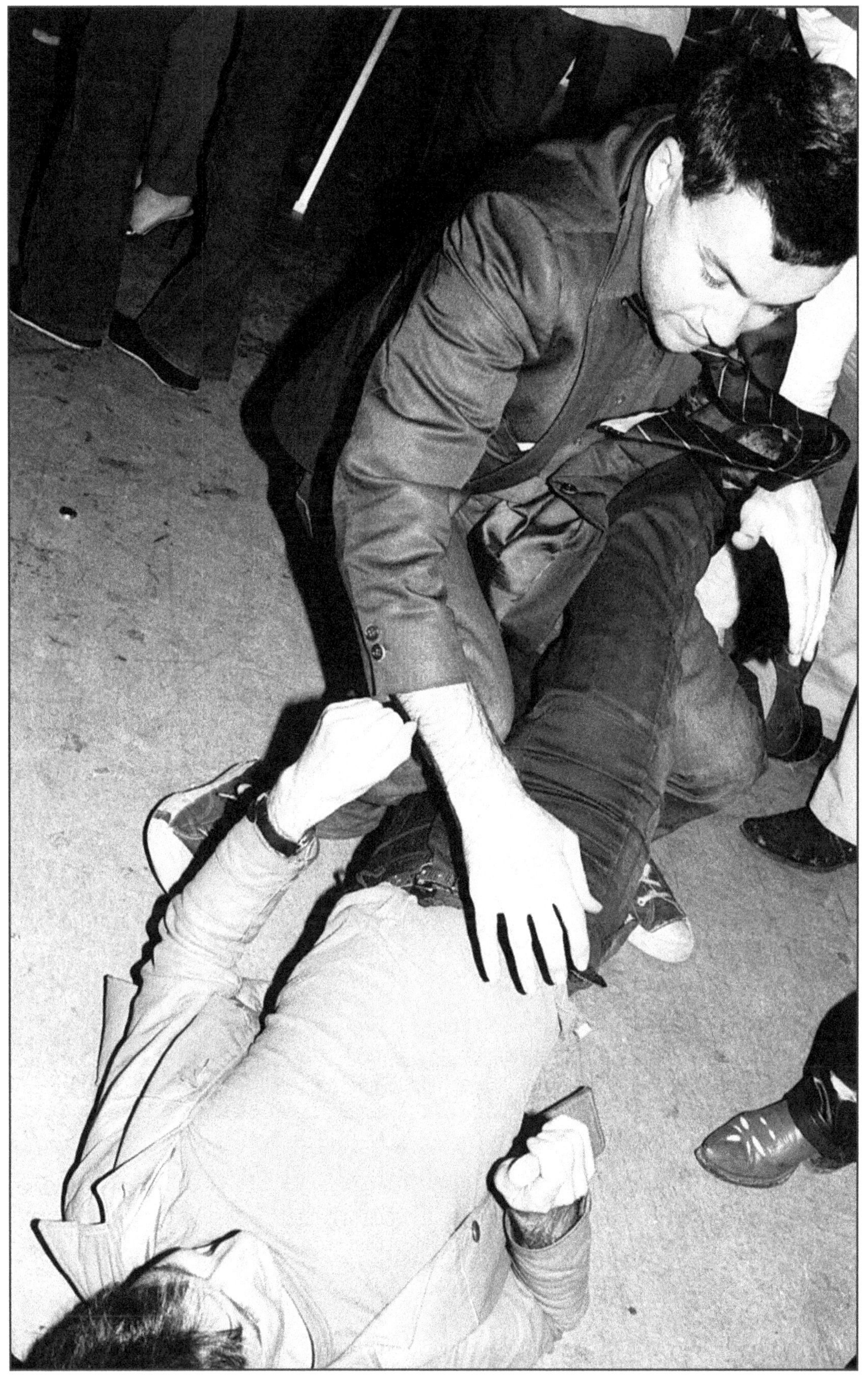

Diego Cortez, curator of the PS 1 art exhibit, wrestling with Victor Bokris, author, at a party an Maripol's loft.

L>R: Johnny Dynell, DJ, Madoka Takagi, photographer and my assistant, Walter Steding, musician and Fred Schneider, poet and "B52s'" frontman.

Victor Bokris, author of a Warhol biography.

George Whipple, photographer.

I have never seen his work printed.

Chris Carroll, photographer, came to show me his portfolio at SPIN telling me he was the world's best photographer. He didn't know who he was talking to. After I left SPIN, he took over as photo editor.

Joe Stevens, photographer and Sue Commings, writer at party for SPIN magazine.

Julia Roberts and Brian Saltern at Area.

Iman, the famous model who became David Bowie's wife and her bodyguards...

Keith Strickland, the "B52s'" drummer playing an Etch-a-Sketch.

Mark Balet "Interview" magazine's art director
and Lisa Robinson, who discovered the Ramones.

Lenny Ferraro and Alexis at Area.

Anton Corbijn, "Ze Famous" Dutch music photographer and film director. Here at the Earl McGrath Gallery for the "Blank Generation Revisited" photo exhibit.

Here is my cousin, Captain Peter Wilkinson, USA in front of two of my photos at the Earl McGrath show for “Blank Generation Revisited”.

Bobby Grossman, the photographer for Glenn O'Brien's "TV Party" cable show. Here at the Earl McGrath Gallery's exhibit of the "Blank Generaton Revisited".

Two photographers, Curtis Knapp and the author.
Curtis is an amazing illustrator, but followed photography.

L>R: Dominic Dreyfus, Danny Newberg, gallerist, Jessica Blue, Yuki Watanabe, facilitator and nightclub owner, and Juliet Dreyfus at Studio 54.

A colleague of mine who also worked
with London Features Internaional.

Robin Platzer, photographer and documentarian
of NY Nightlife.

Patrick Willard, a Frenchman who doubled as an American football announcer for French TV and a NY nightclub DJ.

Patrick spinning at the club Area.

David had wild career swings from leading the "NY Dolls" to doing jazz numbers.

Buster Poindexter aka David Johansen

Vito Bruno, club owner and Aleph, doorman extraordinaire.

Josh Cheuse, once my assistant, then became a big honcho at Sony Music.

Chris Goss, the leader of the band, “Masters of Reality”.
Don’t know the grimace.

Fred Schneider, muscian and Tama Janowitz, writer.

Mahan and Luca Bonetti.

Barbara Egan and the author. I lived in that silver silk suit.

George Rush, writer at Area.

Michael McLintock, actor and musician. R.I.P.

Cheryl Tiegs, Richard Weisman and friend.

Diane Brill and Mark Kostabi, artist.

Fred Schneider on the beach in Bridgehampton, NY.
He liked the beach there and bought a house.

Jean-Michel Basquiat.

Anita Sarko, DJ and Steven Sabin, writer, mesmerized by something?

“The New York City Breakers” wowing the Club NY crowd in Boston.

“The New York City Breakers” showing their stuff to the crowd
at Club NY in Boston.

Once a month, Yuki and Michael O'Brien would bring to Boston, the newest of the new acts coming up in NYC. Madonna, Man Parrish, "Soul Sonic Force" were some of the artists. I tried to book Klaus Nomi, but he was too ill.

L>R: Tom di Pascale, Michael O'Brian and Yuki Watanabe were the organizers of Club NY in Boston.

After Madonna's first Boston concert, I took this photo backstage.

Madonna asked me, "What are you doing here?"
I told her, "I got you the gig..."

I had taken Yuki and Michael to the rooftop at Danceteria, NYC to see her first performance without the "Breakfast Club" only music tracks and her dancers.

L>R" Yuki Watanabe, Bagz Rylez, Martin Burgoyne (Madonna's manager), Michael O'Brien, Madonna, Erika Belle, Christopher Ciccone and Patrick Lyons, the owner of the disco.

Rudolf Piper, principal of Danceteria and Mars.

Big Joe,
two fisted drinker.

Andy on his way to the Whitney Tower wedding.

Fred Hughes was the head of the sales department for Andy Warhol's paintings. Here he looks like Johnny Walker. Perfectly dressed down to his spats.

Bob Guccione, Jr., the publisher of SPIN magazine.

Arthur Weinstein (center), a principal in several clubs, wore a wire for the FBI during an investigation of the Mafia's influence in NYC clubs only to find out how many of the NYPD were corrupt.

David Godlis being filmed at a “Blank Generation Revisited” photo exhibit at the Earl McGrath gallery.

Don't know where or when this picture was taken
of this nice looking lady.

Robert Hayes, the editor of “Interview” magazine
and his sister, Holly at Limelight.

Fran Lebowitz, a writer and frequent contributor to "Interview".
I photographed her several times out and about, but she never smiled.

Nile Rodgers, August Darnell and Joe Jackson.
Backstage, but I don't remember whose show it was.

Real brothers Jeff and Mitchell Hyman
aka Joey Ramone and Mickey Leigh.

Frank Zappa, musician. I can't remember if he was either watching the "B52s" or Klaus Nomi at Irving Plaza, NY.

John Cale, musician and Lisa Robinson, talent scout.

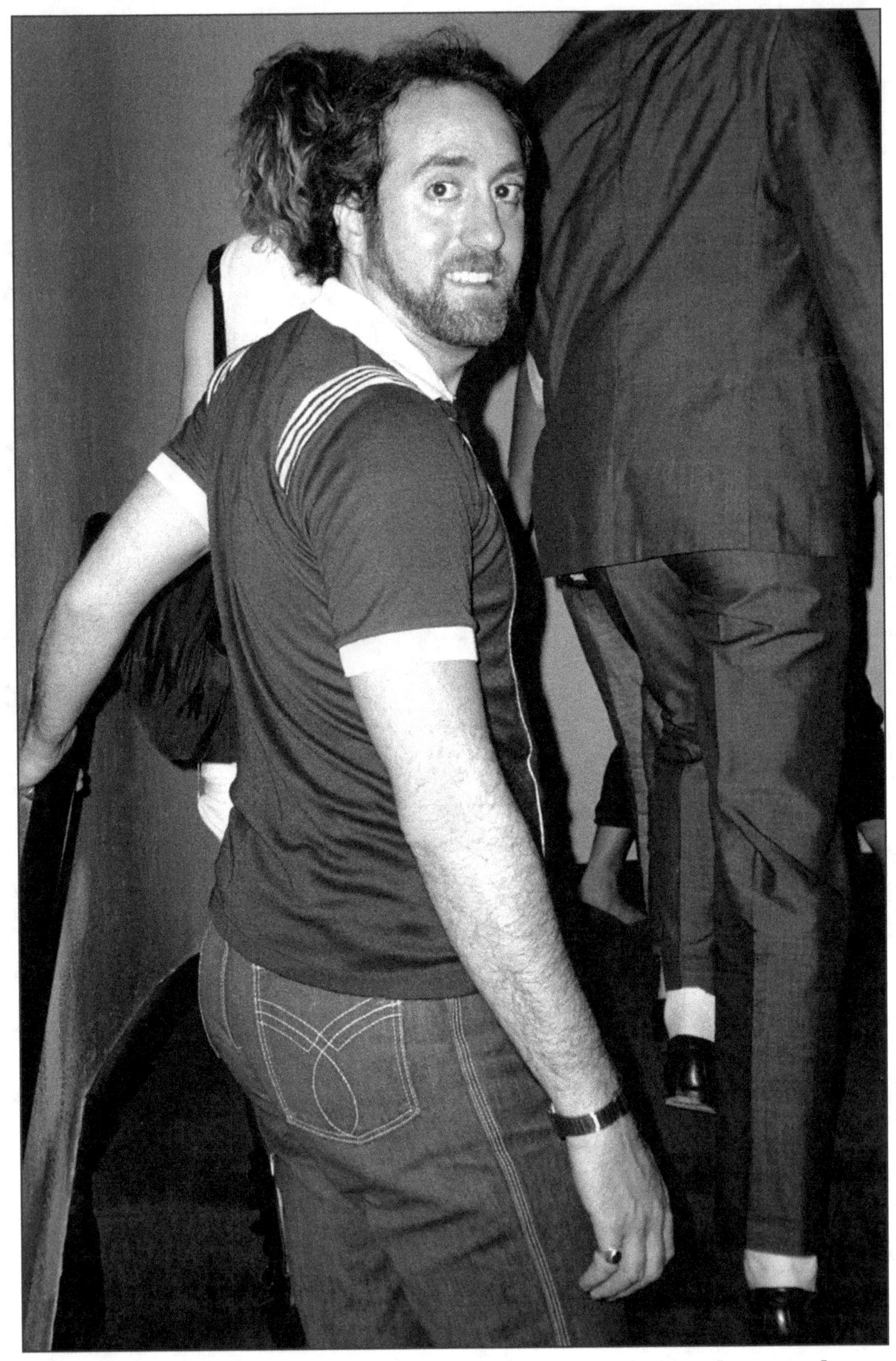

Monte A. Melnick, the Ramones tour manager and wrangler.

Kip Kuba aka Gregory Ambrose Pittman
One of the best rock lyricists of the 21st century.
Search "Gregory's Funhouse"!

David Lichtenstein in the "dressing" room at CBGBs. The whole club's walls were covered with posters and graffiti.

David, gwenl and his father Roy after a performance of David's band, "Cowboy Mouth" at CBGBs.

The staff of SPIN magazine on stage at CBGBs.
We called ourselves "The Ravens".
L>R: Scott Cohen, writer, Mark Weinberg, art director,
Glenn O'Brien, writer and the author on bass.

"The Ravens" in the CBGBs dressing room.Obviously, this photograph was NOT taken by the author, but I have the films.
L>R: Scott, Mark, Glenn and moi.

LAST WORD

Why are there so many photos of certain people? Well, that's because I am basically shy. I never was comfortable taking photos of people that I didn't know. Glenn O'Brien was a good friend of mine, we ran in the same circles, had many common friends and enjoyed the same evening environments. Glenn was also a great Trivial Pursuit player. Rudolf Piper was also a very friendly public person, running Danceteria and Mars clubs in Manhattan. Rudolf's gal pal, Diane Brill was also very personable and friendly.

The night life in Manhattan from the late 70s to the early 80s was quite exciting. Punk and New Wave bands played in CBGBs, Danceteria and sometimes even Studio 54 had live entertainment. The clubs were full from 11pm to 4 in the morning, many of the crowd were either un- or under employed or like me, went home after the day's work, took a "disco nap" and then went out club-hopping and then took the rest of the nap when coming home from the clubs. I am sure there were occasions where I showed up at my photo assistant's job still buzzed.

There maybe people I have misidentified or put them in the wrong club. I tried to solicit help from my other "victims", but this is the best we could do.

I am lucky to have survived such an exciting era and have this book's images to remind me of my luck.

MORE READING

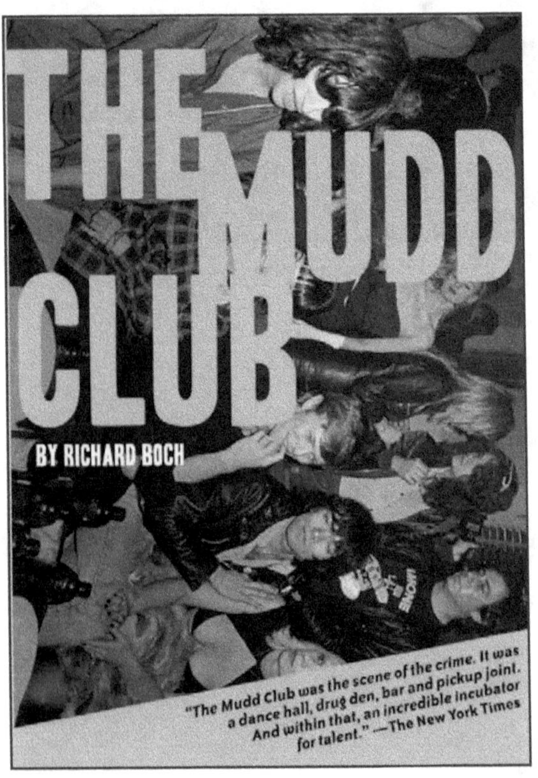

The Mudd Club Paperback – Illustrated, September 12, 2017
by Richard Boch (Author)
ISBN-13: 978-1627310512

"More than the well-known doorman of the Mudd Club, Richard Boch played a pivotal role in why it was the coolest club in the world back then. Richard was the crowd curator, carefully letting in the right mix of wildly creative downtown movers and shakers who made it our hangout, leaving the squares and the unhip outside in the cold. Richard is now letting everyone into the Mudd Club by way of this well written book that details the who's who and all the fun we had while infiltrating, changing and disrupting pop culture." – Fab 5 Freddy

ACKNOWLEDGEMENTS

First, I would like to thank Lane Pederson and Jim Erwin, the photographers who first hired me on a full-time basis, allowed me total access to their studio after hours, use of their Nikons and Hasselblads and oversaw the development of my career and portfolio. I was lucky to have two mentors who were so encouraging.

Eric Boman, R.I.P., who taught me how important hospitality was in encouraging his clients to return for his wonderful lunches. He also taught me some unusual lighting techniques.

Sue Absurd aka Tony Wright, who bought my pre-existing self-commissioned image of the "B52s" and used it for their debut album cover. Tony also gave me many other photo assignments and then got me to work at Island Records, NY as an art director.

Michael Zilkha, the boss at ZE Records for giving me so many cover assignments.

Dee Joseph and Lenny Fichtelberg for letting me photograph and design album covers for so many of their Cold Chillin' artists.

Kathy Schenker, the national publicist for A&M Records for discovering me at the Mudd Club the night that Joe Jackson made his US debut and then giving me so many assignments.

Glenn O'Brien, who used my first "B52s'" photo for his music column at "Interview" magazine, then conning me to come work at SPIN magazine as an art director, then better suited as the photo editor. Glenn was a good friend and we shared a beach house one summer. Glenn also kindly wrote the forewords to two of my books for free. When I wanted to finally pay him for his contribution, he had passed away.

John Cummings aka Johnny Ramone, who gave me album cover and publicity photo assignments for 12 years, calling me on occasion "the official Ramones photographer". I know his loyalty stemmed from his abhorrence of photo shootings and that I could keep these photo sessions extremely short.

Kevin Tooley, for letting me design two of my best album covers for The Hotheads. "World Wide Vibe" and "Landmines", check them out.

Jean Caffiene, Maripol, Yuki Watanabe, Sally Randall Brugen for help with the identifications in this foggy past.

www.ingramcontent.com/pod-product-compliance
Lightning Source LLC
LaVergne TN
7061202120826
149LV00011B/1883